Above left:
The East Lancs bodywork of the Merseyside VRT/LHs lacked the subtle styling of ECW products. Rather than including the engine compartment within the overall body shape, it was constructed to produce an Atlantean-style engine bustle. This was achieved by adding a 'lid' to the Bristol-built moulded fibreglass engine cover which, in the case of VRT/LHs, contained a Gardner 6LXB unit. The position of the second exit door behind the front axle also resulted in both fuel tanks being located on the offside of these buses. No 2031 (UKD 525H) stands here at Liverpool Pier Head. *M. S. Curtis*

Above right:
The lower saloon interior of an ECW-bodied ultra-low VRT/SL. Standard low height bodywork had a completely flat lower deck floor, but the ultra-low version had a slightly sunken gangway – reminiscent of early Bristol Lodekkas. *M. S. Curtis*

Below:
A shiny new VRT3 chassis climbs Brislington Hill at speed during May 1976 as it commences its long drive to the bodybuilder. The sight of Bristol chassis (often driven in convoys), with their drivers exposed to the elements, had been a feature of Brislington life for more than half a century and was greatly missed when the Bristol works eventually closed in 1983. *M. S. Curtis*

Bottom:
A scene inside Eastern Coach Works during August 1971 with a Bristol VRT (centre), a Standerwick VRL coach (extreme right) and several Bristol RE single-deckers with bodywork in the course of construction. *M. S. Curtis*

Martin S. Curtis MCIT, M Inst TA

BRISTOL VR

IAN ALLAN Publishing

Contents

First published 1994

ISBN 0 7110 2238 0

Designed by Ian Allan Studio

Published by
Ian Allan Publishing
an imprint of Ian Allan Ltd, Terminal House, Station Approach, Shepperton, Surrey TW17 8AS; and printed by Ian Allan Printing Ltd, Coombelands House, Coombelands Lane, Addlestone, Surrey KT15 1HY.

Previous page:
East Kent reverted to its traditional burgundy and cream when released from NBC corporate livery policy, but applied in a revised layout. No 7982 (TFN 982T), here accelerating away from Folkestone bus station, was a surviving VRT/SL3/6LXB with the comparatively rare Willowbrook bodywork when photographed during June 1991. *M. S. Curtis*

Introduction

If asked to portray the 'Bristol VR', those professionally engaged in the bus industry, together with interested followers of the road passenger transport scene, would almost certainly convey an image of a highly standardised, ECW-bodied 70-75-seat double-decker, powered by a transversely-mounted rear engine – and probably finished in either red or green NBC livery.

It would be correct to say that this is how the Bristol VR is usually visualised, but it began as a very different passenger chassis design, which was not only original and innovative, but offered a seemingly endless range of body design possibilities.

The VR was the last of a long line of double-deck bus chassis to be built entirely in the City of Bristol. It was conceived during the mid-1960s, at a time when considerable excitement surrounded the activities of Bristol Commercial Vehicles Ltd, which had already produced such august models as the Bristol Lodekka and Bristol RE, both of which rapidly established new design standards for the passenger transport industry. The Bristol company had also just been freed from burdensome sales restrictions, its products becoming universally available once more after an absence, in some markets, of almost 20 years. The release of another new Bristol chassis against this background could not fail to attract tremendous interest, and was eagerly awaited.

The first ever Bristol double-decker appeared in 1923, to be followed by a series of highly successful designs which culminated in Bristol's lowheight Lodekka – which was nothing short of revolutionary in concept. Bristol's approach to the original VR design was equally unconventional.

I vividly recall seeing the green Bristol Omnibus-liveried VR prototype for the first time, when it just happened to be parked outside my Brislington home one Sunday afternoon in 1966. Its layout was drastically different from any previous Bristol (or even the Leyland Atlantean) and there was an air of great excitement about its appearance. Its classic ECW body styling combined a traditional reassurance with dynamic modernity, yet the whole look of this vehicle seemed to be 'just right'.

No one could then have doubted that the VR would be another great success for Bristol and Eastern Coach Works and there was certainly no lack of confidence from its manufacturers. But, alas, almost as soon as the prototypes commenced operational trials, the course of British bus manufacturing changed, with politics and revised legislation combining with a tendency among some operators to be cautious about introducing this untried configuration. The Bristol VR was accordingly forced to change direction hurriedly in order to keep pace with events.

It was hastily redesigned, to produce a chassis incorporating an entirely new engine position for Bristol, following the layout of its rival models. Unfortunately the new variant (to be known as the VRT) lacked the benefit of thorough research and testing as applied to previous Bristol designs – and consequently it faltered. Indeed, it was effectively banished completely from Scotland until quite recently!

Meanwhile, the company persevered with the original design (with side-mounted, rear engine) for a little longer, as the VRL, but it soon became clear that there was insufficient demand to justify continued production of this version. It remains a matter of great regret that this ingenious layout was never allowed to realise its full potential. Instead, Bristol accepted the already established pattern of placing the engine across the rear of the chassis. The necessary corrections and improvements to the VRT followed as rapidly as possible, which allowed its reputation to recover, but only gradually.

During this era, conversion of services to one-person operation was sweeping the country, both to improve productivity and to alleviate chronic staff shortages in many areas. Bristol's rear-engined double-decker therefore became synonymous with such conversions that accelerated its introduction into a number of fleets.

Eventually, the VR's fortunes were turned around and it went on to become Britain's top-selling double-decker! No doubt its most popular power unit, the legendary Gardner diesel engine, assisted in this respect, since this proven and economical unit was highly regarded among transport operators.

The success of the VR also depended largely on the loyalty of its customers. Bristol Commercial Vehicles was never short of support from operators. When one reflects on the major upheavals to which the British bus industry has been subjected since the VR was introduced, the continued prominence of this bus suggests that, in the end, the Bristol designers produced a vehicle which possessed considerable versatility and durability. As a result it has survived a succession of major and largely unforeseen changes to the structure and control of road passenger transport.

The Bristol VR appears set to continue in service for many more years, although for many of us it is a matter of eternal sorrow that Bristol Commercial Vehicles no longer exists to continue production of road passenger chassis. This volume, recalling the last double-decker regularly to carry the 'Bristol' name, is therefore an appropriate tribute to those responsible for its design and production.

Acknowledgements

A book such as this attempts to capture an accurate and balanced record – together with something of the spirit – of the vehicle it portrays. This can never be achieved by one person alone, and I have therefore relied heavily on the assistance and support of many individuals and organisations in order to provide comprehensive coverage of each variant, at the same time reflecting the wide range of customers for this model.

This is my fourth book to recall aspects of Bristol vehicle history, and the Bristol VR is a subject I have been eager to see covered for some years. Nevertheless, production of this volume would not have been possible without the generosity, interest and enthusiasm of a great many friends and colleagues, together with the equally important assistance from enthusiasts, and professionals from within the bus industry – including of course those employed by Bristol Commercial Vehicles and Eastern Coach Works.

In particular, I would like to thank Allan Macfarlane and Michael Tozer, both acknowledged Bristol experts who share my enthusiasm for Brislington-built vehicles. They, once again, checked the draft text, and their advice and suggestions have been invaluable.

Additional material has also been provided by: Allen Janes (who continues to research Bristol's earliest history), Ken Horler and Paul Davies of Badgerline (Bath) engineering, the journals *Buses* and *Motor Transport (Bus & Coach)*, The PSV Circle and Omnibus Society, the late John B. Appleby, G. Bond of Leyland Bus, Geoff Bruce, Viv Carter of Carter's Coaches, Steve Chislett, Maurice Doggett, Alan Dorrington of the Dept of Transport, Allan Field, Peter Gascoine, Tony Hall, Sgt Mark Hughes of Devizes Police Driving School, David Hunt, Brian Jackson, Dennis Lane, Lowland Omnibuses Ltd, Garry Mears, Stephen Morris, D. H. Parker, A. Alan Townsin, Greg Travers and Mike Walker.

The overwhelming generosity of photographers who responded to my requests for illustrations deserves special mention, and views appear by courtesy of the individual or organisation whose name is credited against each caption.

Finally, I extend special thanks to my wife Julie, who (as with my previous two books) undertook the typing of manuscripts. She, together with my children, Thomas and Leanne, also tolerated numerous excursions in pursuit of Bristol VR material while enduring disruption to their domestic lives – which have largely revolved around publishing deadlines during the many months of preparation and assembly of this book.

Martin S. Curtis
Warmley,
Bristol
Summer 1993

1

VR Ancestry

When Bristol Commercial Vehicles began exploring ideas for the design of a new passenger model in the early 1960s, it had established a reputation as a producer of among the most reliable and innovative bus and coach chassis in the country. In production at that time was a range of passenger chassis suitable for both single- and double-deck bodywork, together with heavy goods vehicle chassis, but supplies of vehicles from Bristol's factories at Brislington, in the southeast of the city, were restricted to the state-owned transport undertakings.

The first ever 'Bristol' bus was a 16-seater, assembled in 1908 by the Bristol Tramways & Carriage Co Ltd for use on its own services, in the period when motorised road transport was still in its infancy.

Whilst convinced there was enormous potential for motor vehicles, the Bristol Tramways company had not been impressed with at least some of the models it had already operated and set about designing and building buses to its own specification. This, in turn, led to increased production and sales to other operators with many chassis appearing with goods, rather than passenger, bodywork. Increasingly, however, the design emphasis of the company's products moved towards passenger chassis and in 1923 the first Bristol double-deckers appeared, based on the 4-ton chassis.

Two years later, in 1925, Bristol unveiled its A-type model (commencing a series of model designations in alphabetical sequence). This was a purpose-built heavyweight passenger chassis with low frame and driving position alongside the engine, equally suitable for either double- or single-deck bodywork.

Further double-deck models followed throughout the 1920s and 1930s including the C-type six-wheeler with twin rear axles, the G-type which was available with either diesel or more traditional petrol engines, and the K-type. The Bristol K (like its single-deck equivalent the L-type) was entirely diesel powered, with most engines built either by Gardner of Manchester or, from the 1940s, Bristol itself.

Bristol Tramways & Carriage Co Ltd became a member of the Tilling group of companies from the early 1930s, and although Bristol's own coachworks continued in production for a further quarter of a century, there followed a close association with another Tilling company, Eastern Coach Works Ltd of Lowestoft. Together, Bristol and ECW became the main suppliers of vehicles to the whole Tilling group. Neither company was restricted to building in conjunction with the other nor were they prevented from accepting orders from outside the Tilling organisation; indeed this was encouraged, and in the 1940s considerable export success was achieved. K-type double-deck production had totalled over 4,100 when this model was withdrawn in 1957, Bristol by then having firmly established an enviable reputation for quality and reliability.

In 1948, the M-type chassis for either single- or double-deck bodywork had been announced, but this design did not progress

Above:
The first vehicles ever built by Bristol were 16-seat C40-types which entered service in May 1908. For many years it was believed that the initial batch comprised five vehicles registered AE771-AE775 and allocated stock numbers from 97 onwards. However, this recently rediscovered photograph of No 96 (AE770) suggests an earlier, sixth, C40 existed, and that probably this was the first Bristol ever to be constructed. *Bristol Vintage Bus Group (BVBG)*

Right:
Bristol's first chassis to receive double-deck bodywork appeared in 1923 when a batch of nine such vehicles, based on the company's 4-ton chassis, was built for Hull Corporation. Among them was AT 7355, fitted with 53-seat Dick Kerr bodywork, operating here among tramcars while destined for Stoneferry.
M. J. Tozer collection

Right:
Bristol introduced its K-type double-decker in 1937, and several hundred were rapidly added to its own fleet, including a large number for tram replacement in the City of Bristol itself. Bodywork orders were divided between the company's Brislington bodybuilding works and Eastern Coach Works, one of the latter being this K5G model, C3296 (GAE 494), photographed shortly after the outbreak of war in 1939.
Eastern Coach Works

beyond the prototype stage. A year later, however, Bristol's next double-deck chassis was to revolutionise British double-decker design. This was the Bristol Lodekka (Low Decker) model which successfully overcame the problems of constructing a double-decker (for routes which required high capacity vehicles) within an overall height limit of 13ft 6in. This was essential for many operators, whose buses had to pass under the numerous railway bridges and other obstructions found throughout the country. A standard double-decker was some 12in taller at 14ft 6in, and this difference was often critical. The established solution to reducing height before the Lodekka appeared was to build a 'lowbridge' body with a sunken gangway on the extreme offside of the upper saloon with four abreast seating for top-deck passengers. This arrangement was both uncomfortable and awkward for upper-deck passengers and caused fare collection difficulties for conductors, while the sunken gangway reduced headroom for passengers below. The Lodekka swept away these problems as it allowed a traditional centre gangway and standard headroom on both decks while the overall height of the bus was equivalent to that of a lowbridge vehicle. Moreover, the lower-deck floor was virtually flat, with no step from the rear platform into the lower saloon – providing further benefits. To achieve this, Bristol and ECW worked closely together to develop a chassis with an offset drive line running along the offside of the chassis, which followed trials with split transmission arrangements in the early prototypes. This in turn led to a new design of dropped-centre rear axle which, together with down-swept chassis cross-members, allowed the creation of a semi-integral vehicle with the lower-deck floor and body framing directly attached to the chassis. With an exceptionally low bottom-deck floor, the height of the remainder of the body was accordingly reduced.

The Lodekka was produced in various forms, including forward entrance versions until September 1968, by which date over 5,200 had been built. Although the Lodekka was quickly established as a most successful model, Bristol was prevented from freely supplying it to operators because both Bristol and ECW were nationalised in 1948 when the Tilling group sold its bus interests to the state.

As a result, neither Bristol nor ECW was permitted to accept further orders from operators outside the state-owned transport groups, much to the despair of many operators who were loyal to Bristol and ECW, and wanted to operate models such as the Lodekka.

Not surprisingly, several other manufacturers produced their own versions of low-height double-deckers following the Lodekka's lead, but few were as successful as the Bristol design, and some were spectacular disasters!

However, in the mid-1950s an agreement was reached with Dennis Bros of Guildford to build the Lodekka under licence as the Dennis Loline, which at least gave non-nationalised operators the chance to share the benefits of the Lodekka concept.

Among other manufacturers working on their own design of low-height double-decker was Leyland Motors, which had been studying an alternative method of dealing with the lowheight problem. By 1954, two Leyland Lowloader prototypes had been completed. Like the original Lodekkas, they featured rear-entrance lowheight bodywork with a conventional seating layout incorporating central gangways on both decks. However, unlike the Bristol Lodekka with its engine alongside the driver in the conventional position, the Lowloader's engine was placed transversely across the rear of the bus. This represented a major departure from established practice, but although the engine used was a compact turbo-charged unit, the conflict between passenger flows and engine location on the rear platform was undoubtedly one factor which resulted in no further production versions following. Nevertheless, Leyland had established the principle of placing an engine across the rear of a double-deck bus and two years later it revealed its Atlantean model, which not only featured a rear-mounted engine (and semi-automatic transmission) but also a set-back front axle ahead of which was the passenger entrance at the side – and under the full control – of the driver. With a staircase immediately behind the driver's cab, a new standard layout for double-deckers was in the making. Ironically early production Atlanteans could not be built in lowheight form without reverting to the unpopular 'lowbridge' layout with side-gangway for the rearmost area of the upper deck! The Atlantean layout was nevertheless

Below:
The revolutionary Bristol Lodekka was unveiled in 1949 when LHY 949, the first prototype, was completed. It became C5000 in the Bristol City fleet and spent much of its life operating, as here, on service 36 before this outstanding vehicle was withdrawn in 1963 and scrapped. However, it set standards which were to later influence the Bristol VR, and successive chassis designs. *BVBG*

Above:
Bristol Omnibus took the extraordinary step (for a Tilling company) of introducing three Leyland Atlanteans in 1963. They were purchased from Wilts & Dorset which had just acquired them with the business of Silver Star of Porton Down. Despite wearing standard Tilling green and cream livery, their appearance was radically different from the company's otherwise highly standardised Bristol double-deckers and, being of lowheight design, featured a lowbridge seating arrangement with side gangway at the rear of the top deck. Emerging here from Bristol's Marlborough Street bus and coach station is No 7999 (1013 MW), heading for Weston-super-Mare on service 24, one of the routes regularly worked by the Atlanteans until their withdrawal after only a year. *BVBG*

to influence Bristol's designers, and those of other vehicle builders, in future years.

Production Atlanteans became increasingly familiar throughout the country from 1958 with their flat fronts and power units housed inside a characteristic engine 'bustle' protruding from the rear. In 1960 a rival to the Atlantean appeared on the scene in the form of Daimler's Fleetline double-deck chassis. The Fleetline followed the same basic layout as the Atlantean but offered operators the choice of a Gardner engine, and central-gangway lowheight bodywork by using a dropped-centre rear axle which had still to appear as an option on production Atlanteans.

Competition between the Atlantean and Fleetline became intense, and large numbers entered service with British Electric Traction group companies together with municipalities and some independents. London Transport also took trial batches of both types while, significantly, the Fleetline found favour with the nationalised Scottish Bus Group, which could and did also purchase Bristol-built vehicles.

Both Leyland and Daimler continued also to produce conventional front-engined double-deckers throughout this period, with Daimler finding itself under British Leyland ownership by 1968. Despite this, Daimler's Fleetline continued to compete actively for business against the Atlantean (together with, by this time, a third newly-released, rear-engined model which had rather hurriedly made its début). Simultaneously, it was evident that many operators were moving away from double-deckers for use on urban services in favour of saloons, although this trend was to be short-lived.

Returning to Bristol products, the company's single-deck designs of the 1950s were less revolutionary than the Lodekka, but again major design changes occurred, with horizontal underfloor engines becoming established for bus and coach use alike. Most manufacturers were following this fashion and Bristol had built three main designs to this layout by the early 1960s: the LS, MW and SU-types.

By 1962 Bristol once more set design standards that the rest of the industry would have to follow when it launched its RE (Rear Engine) single-deck chassis. This used the dropped-centre rear axle from the Lodekka and featured an underfloor engine mounted behind the rear axle instead of the (by then) accepted amidships position, and a front-mounted radiator. A very low entrance at the front could be achieved by this arrangement on bus versions with the elimination of the steep steps needed to reach high floor levels on other underfloor-engine models, while the area between the axles could accommodate luggage lockers on coach versions with higher frames. Again, other manufacturers followed this layout, but the RE was easily the most successful of the first generation of rear-engined single-deckers.

During the 1950s, and while remaining nationalised under the British Transport Commission, the Bristol Tramways & Carriage Co Ltd title was lost when first the bus manufacturing department of the Bristol company was separated from the bus operating section to become Bristol Commercial Vehicles Ltd in 1955, to be followed two years later by the operating Bristol company itself being renamed Bristol Omnibus Company Ltd. Nevertheless, and as one might have expected, strong links remained between the two companies and both continued to use the 'Bristol' scroll emblem.

In 1963, the British Transport Commission was succeeded by the Transport Holding Co, though this made little visible difference to Bristol or ECW. By 1965, however, another change in ownership was greatly to affect production as arrangements were made for the Leyland Motor Corporation to take a 25% stake in the bus manufacturing activities at Bristol and Lowestoft.

This immediately released both Bristol Commercial Vehicles and Eastern Coach Works from sales restrictions, once more allowing the companies to supply any customer, either as partners or separately. With models such as the Lodekka and RE already well established as pace-setters in the manufacturing business, the bus industry watched with great expectation to see what next would emerge from the factories of Bristol and ECW.

Below:
The Daimler Fleetline followed a generally similar layout to the Atlantean, including a rear bustle containing a transversely-mounted engine. This Fleetline carries a style of ECW bodywork derived from that designed for the Bristol VRT, and which looks all the more Tilling-like finished in a livery of Lothian green — the name given to Tilling green when applied to vehicles of Scottish Omnibuses Ltd. It is numbered DD709 (KSX 709N) and was built in 1975. *M. S. Curtis*

2

From Drawing Board to Prototypes

Throughout 1965, the Bristol and ECW design teams explored new and varied vehicle design possibilities with a view to offering a modern and extremely competitive range of passenger models in the open market.

In the short term, consideration was given to expanding the existing range of models with, among the proposals, a Lodekka that would be capable of taking standard-height bodywork – not necessarily built by ECW. This followed plans for a double-deck RE with rear underfloor engine, and consideration was also given to a model with a horizontal engine positioned under the driver's cab. Considerable importance was attached to the principle of offering operators a high degree of standardisation within their fleets, with basically similar chassis being available for double-deck, single-deck or coaching roles.

It was recognised that in the longer term, entirely new models would be needed to meet not only the requirements of the nationalised Tilling and Scottish groups but also other operators whose custom Bristol and ECW were anxious to attract. In response to these demands, the designers' attention was directed towards a new lowheight chassis. This was to be designated type 'N' (thereby reviving the alphabetical sequence that had been last used in 1948 – more recent Bristols having had letter codes which reflected characteristics of their design) and a small single-deck chassis, possibly with a rear engine, for lightweight duties (to be the P-type).

By the summer of 1965 quite detailed proposals existed for the N-type. This vehicle was to be one of the most potentially versatile British PSVs ever built and Bristol had again arrived at an ingenious solution to meet the requirements for either bus or coach work, by locating the engine longitudinally at the rear offside of the chassis. With a choice of at least two chassis lengths, this allowed any combination of passenger entrance doors on the nearside – ahead of the front axle, within the wheelbase or behind the rear wheels – while double-deckers could accommodate stairs anywhere along the offside behind the driver's cab, and the possibility for a long, large-capacity vehicle with passenger doors

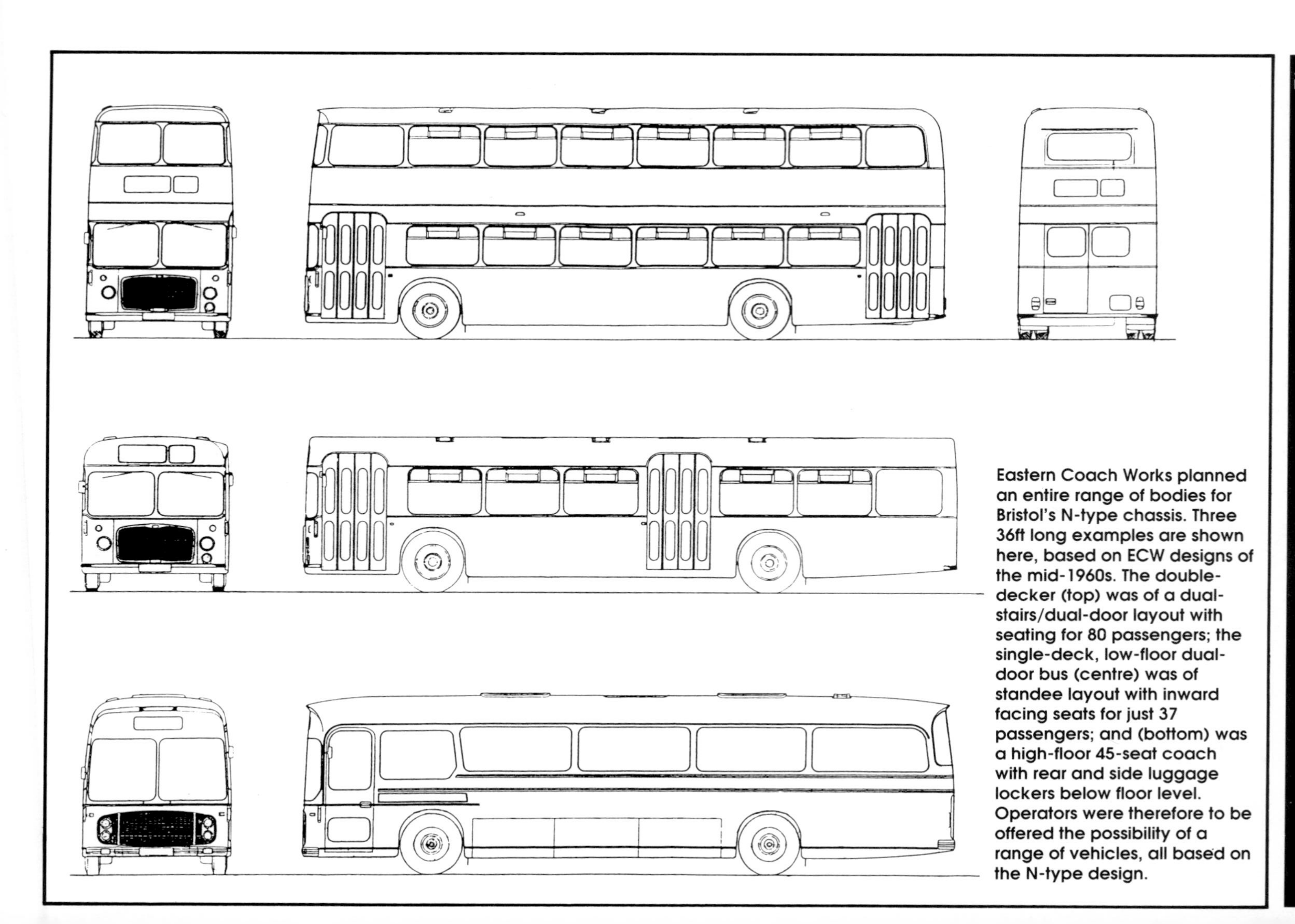

Eastern Coach Works planned an entire range of bodies for Bristol's N-type chassis. Three 36ft long examples are shown here, based on ECW designs of the mid-1960s. The double-decker (top) was of a dual-stairs/dual-door layout with seating for 80 passengers; the single-deck, low-floor dual-door bus (centre) was of standee layout with inward facing seats for just 37 passengers; and (bottom) was a high-floor 45-seat coach with rear and side luggage lockers below floor level. Operators were therefore to be offered the possibility of a range of vehicles, all based on the N-type design.

Above:
Bristol's N-type experimental prototype, NX. 001, was the first chassis built to the design which was to become known as the Bristol VR. It is shown shortly after completion in 1966. With Long wheelbase and Low frame, and powered by a Gardner 6LX engine mounted longitudinally in the rear offside corner of the chassis, it corresponded with what would later be known as VRL/LL specification. Such a chassis would have been suitable for 36ft (11m) long bodywork, but this particular example was never bodied, and remained unique. It stands here at BCV's Bath Road (Top) works with the company's Ford Anglia van behind. *Motor Transport – Bus & Coach*

and stairs at both the front and rear was among the options for which detailed designs were in hand.

These exciting design possibilities became clearer as three detailed chassis type proposals were defined as follows: NDL for N-type, Double-deck, Long wheelbase suitable for bodywork of 36ft (11m) length; NDS for bodywork as above but with Shorter wheelbase offering an overall length of some 32ft 6in (10m); and NS for Single-deck use carrying either low-floor bus or high-floor coach bodywork, again with an overall length of 36ft (11m).

It was not until the summer of 1966 that the first prototype N-type chassis was revealed as experimental chassis No NX.001. This was a long version with 18ft 6in wheelbase intended for 36ft (11m)-long bodywork with a low frame and double-reduction, dropped-centre rear axle to allow a double-deck body height of no more than 13ft 6in. It continued the Lodekka concept, although it was planned that additional high-frame versions would be suitable for standard-height bodywork.

Such a chassis would offer operators the opportunity to buy a 36ft double-decker for the first time – accommodating up to 90 seated passengers – although this chassis was equally suited for single-deck coachwork subject to variations in the specification of suspension and road wheels. The longitudinally-mounted engine in NX.001 was a 150bhp Gardner 6LX unit although Leyland-engined versions were also planned for the future. This was coupled to a Self-Changing Gears five-speed epicyclic gearbox, while similar semi-automatic transmissions were simultaneously being introduced as an option for FLF-type Lodekkas and REs.

So great was the versatility of the N-type design that a front entrance vehicle, with or without a centre exit, could be based on this chassis for possible one-man operation. This, whilst becoming widespread on single-deckers, was not legalized for British double-deckers until the time of the N-type's appearance. However, a more traditional approach could also be taken, since the chassis was also suitable for bodywork offering a rear entrance

Right:
An impression by the author of how the Bristol N-type might have looked, based on an Eastern Coach Works drawing (No 4851) of June 1965. Eighty seats were to be contained within this 32ft 7½in-long lowheight body design, which included a peaked front dome, an upright rear dome, curved front windows and frontal styling similar to contemporary designs for RE single-deckers. The original ECW design on which this was based had already been extensively altered to reduce seating capacity and change front and rear styling, and a number of further modifications were made before a body of this layout was approved for the VRX prototypes the following year.

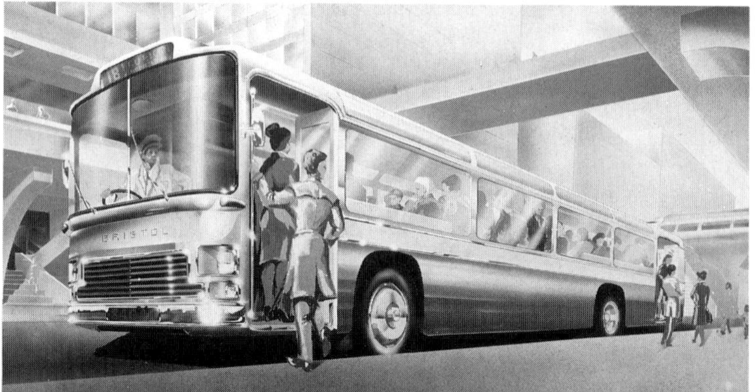

Centre right:
A further artist's impression of an N-type, this time prepared for Bristol Commercial Vehicles and illustrating how a 36ft-long standee city bus with front entrance and rear exit might have looked. Such a vehicle would have been capable of carrying some 70 passengers, half of whom would have had to stand. *Bristol*

Above:
The two VRX prototypes with Short, Low frames became the first VRs to receive bodywork. Here, one of the VRX chassis clearly displays the unobtrusive engine position, dropped-centre rear axle and general chassis arrangement including rear perimeter framing. The fuel tank, at this stage, was still located under the driving position, and power was again provided by a 10.45-litre Gardner 6LX unit. *Bristol*

and platform with staircase rising conventionally (over the engine) on the rear offside corner of the bus.

During the ensuing years, a considerable debate was to follow among operators over the relative merits of crew or one-man operation, and the disadvantages from an engineering viewpoint of placing the engine at the rear (of all makes of chassis), remote from the driver. Engine accessibility on the N-type was excellent, however, with removable body panels planned for the side and rear of the engine compartment externally, and detachable top and side covers internally, allowing access to every area of the power unit. This could be achieved without the need for a pit, representing a considerable improvement over other designs.

The imbalance of weight between offside and nearside caused by the engine location was seen as a problem by some potential operators, but Bristol argued that the camber of most roads tended to place a weight emphasis on the nearside of heavy vehicles which counterbalanced this effect. Furthermore, and as with the Lodekka, the chassis frame itself was designed to be closely integrated with the body sides to support the weight of running units within the complete structure of the vehicle.

Other features of the N-type chassis included a cab comprised of a one-piece draught-free moulded glass fibre unit, with good control and instrument layout, pendant pedals and a well-raked steering wheel similar to the Lodekka. A conventional, mechanical handbrake was employed, but footbrake operation was by a direct-air system (as with the later REs and Lodekkas) with separate systems for front and rear. Despite the engine position, the radiator was mounted at the front of the chassis (in Bristol RE fashion) to take full advantage of the natural air flow of the bus when in motion, while a 36-gallon fuel tank was located below the cab. Suspension, surprisingly, consisted of conventional leaf springs rather than the air suspension offered on other Bristol models.

NX.001, the first prototype chassis, was assembled alongside a second chassis frame of similar design which was never completed, and did not leave the experimental shop before being dismantled. Indeed, even NX.001 never received a body, but within a few months of its appearance two further, similar chassis did receive double-deck bodywork. These were slightly shorter versions with a wheelbase of 16ft 2in rather than 18ft 6in, with length reductions achieved by differences to the chassis frame ahead of the rear axle. In other respects the shorter versions were similar to the first chassis, with power again provided by 10.45-litre Gardner 6LX engines.

At this juncture, Bristol decided to re-designate this model with type letters reflecting characteristics of the chassis. Accordingly, the N-type was henceforth to be known as the Bristol VR (for Vertical Rear engine). The bodied prototypes therefore received chassis Nos VRX.001 and VRX.002 respectively and, with Short wheelbase and Low frame, were constructed to VRSL specification. Bodywork for these two vehicles was produced by Eastern Coach Works (with body Nos EX10 and EX11) and both were to a basically similar front-entrance layout, with rearward ascending stairs and seating for 35 in the lower and 45 in the upper saloons. With the addition of standing passengers, well over 80 passengers could be accommodated within an overall length of 33ft. Despite being of lowheight design, the overall height was almost 13ft 8in – some 3in taller than a Lodekka!

The body design was unmistakably to ECW's styling, with front and rear domes obviously following the pattern set since the 1940s – even though careful consideration had been given to completely revising their design. The body panelling very cleverly concealed the engine location, and unlike other rear-engined double-deckers it was far from obvious, when viewing the exterior, exactly where the engine was located! Inside, an engine cover incorporating a luggage compartment housed the power unit although engine noise levels were perfectly acceptable. Indeed a high-pitched transmission whine – which was becoming characteristic of Bristols of this period – was often more noticeable at higher speeds.

Having a front-mounted radiator, a most attractive grille (in a style that only ECW seemed capable of producing) appeared below the windscreens, and here too was a

Right:
VRX.001, the first of the VR prototypes to receive bodywork, was painted in Central SMT livery as BN331 (GGM 431D). Its new design of ECW bodywork included a very attractive grille and front end, seen for the first time on this vehicle — as was the new 'Bristol VR' badge. However, the traditional scroll emblems were to remain attached firmly to the walls at the main entrance to BCV's Bath Road premises, where GGM 431D prepares to join the main traffic flow as it embarks on a road test. *Motor Transport – Bus & Coach.*

cast 'Bristol VR' badge – which would be followed by similar versions for other Bristol models. This plate included the name 'Bristol' in block letters, which was to be Bristol Commercial Vehicles Ltd's new symbol as it was felt to be more in keeping with the image of a progressive company re-entering the open market, than was the scroll. The same design also appeared on the wheel hubs, steering wheel centre, in publicity material, and eventually over the main doors of Bristol's Chatsworth Road chassis assembly shops. It is interesting that Bristol scroll symbols were however retained on the foot pedals of all production Bristol VRs and that the traditional scroll signs at the entrance to Bristol's main Bath Road works were never replaced!

Bristol and ECW attended the 1966 Commercial Motor Show at Earls Court in September of that year – the first time either company had exhibited at such an event since 1948 because of the restrictions imposed on sales. The occasion offered the opportunity for both VRXs to make their first public appearance and, not surprisingly, they attracted enormous interest.

VRX.001 actually appeared at the exhibition on ECW's stand (alongside a Bristol RE single-decker). It was finished in the deep red and cream livery of Central SMT and carried registration GGM 431D. Internally, the finish was light and airy, setting standards for future VRs, with seats finished in a tartan moquette.

On Bristol's own stand was an RELL chassis and the second VRX (registered HHW 933D). When built, this bus had been completed in full Bristol Omnibus livery of Tilling green with a cream waistband and black wheels and proudly carried the Bristol scroll on its body sides, which Bristol Omnibus had introduced as a fleetname on its vehicles the previous year. By the time it appeared at Earls Court, its wheels had been repainted cream and a transparent panel fitted to display the engine. Internally, the seating layout was identical to the Central SMT vehicle except the finish was much darker with the Bristol Omnibus Co's existing specification of green interior panelling and traditional Tilling group moquette. Despite the respective liveries, both VR prototypes remained the property of Bristol Commercial Vehicles.

By the beginning of 1967 a fourth, completed VR chassis had appeared and once again no bodywork was fitted. Moreover, this vehicle differed from the previous prototypes in a number of respects. Although designed for 36ft-long bodywork, it was built to VRLH (Long, High) specification with the alternative higher chassis frame without outriggers, while power was provided by a Leyland engine. Some redesign work had also taken place around the rear wheel arches, part of the perimeter framing was lost on this version, and spring brake units were also fitted. Nevertheless, the fuel tank remained under the driving

Above:
A rear nearside picture of VRX. 001 on completion of its 80-seat coachwork. In view of the variety of body designs produced at Lowestoft for this type of vehicle, it is interesting to note that the designers had reverted largely to traditional styling for the finished product, retaining many familiar ECW features to produce a clean, well-proportioned finish. Cleverly, the engine location is far from obvious at first glance, although its position necessitated a long rear overhang, limiting the ability to further reduce overall length. *ECW*

Right:
This is the interior lower saloon of GGM 431D, illustrating the compact engine compartment cover which provided a useful luggage stowage area alongside the inward facing bench seat above the wheel-arch. Located to the right is the rear emergency door. *ECW*

Above:
VRX. 002, the second VR prototype to be bodied by ECW, was registered HHW 933D. At first it carried full Bristol Omnibus Co livery, in which condition it is shown here complete with Bristol scroll fleetnames, black wheels and even BOC legal lettering behind the front nearside wheel. It would have been logical for this vehicle to enter trial service with Bristol Omnibus, as so many prototype and experimental Bristol buses had done earlier, but it was to be some years before this bus ran in service with BCV's local operator. *ECW*

Right:
Both VRX prototypes were exhibited at the Commercial Motor Show held at Earls Court during September 1966. HHW 933D formed part of Bristol Commercial Vehicles' own display, still wearing Bristol Omnibus Tilling green livery, but with its wheels repainted cream. In order to emphasise the unorthodox engine position, the engine area was illuminated and could be viewed through a transparent side panel, fitted specially for the occasion. *P. F. Davies*

position and the cab and radiator design was similar to the earlier prototype VRs.

In spite of the release of Bristol's products on the open market, the nationalised fleets continued to represent the main group of customers for Brislington-built buses and coaches. Prior to the VR, prototypes of new Bristol models were usually allocated to operating companies (including, invariably, Bristol itself) and then thoroughly tested with group companies borrowing these vehicles for inspection and evaluation, so as much operational experience as possible was gained before quantity production began. This eliminated many of the teething troubles associated with new vehicle designs but, unfortunately, a slightly different course was followed in the case of the VR. As a result, the VR was denied the opportunity to establish, at an early stage, a reputation for a high degree of reliability – something that had been synonymous with earlier Bristol models.

In January 1967 VRX.001, which had appeared in Central SMT livery at the Commercial Motor Show, was delivered to Central in Motherwell, where it entered service as No BN331 (with the type code perpetuating the Bristol N-type designation!). It was to be retained in Scotland for over three years, and whilst initially allocated to busy urban routes, in due course this bus spent lengthy periods withdrawn from service owing to mechanical difficulties.

Meanwhile, the second prototype had toured several Tilling companies by February 1967, when it was allocated not, as expected, to BCV's local operator Bristol, but instead to Mansfield District Traction Co as No 555. A month later VRX.002 was back in Bristol, where it was given a Gloucester fleetname and coat of arms by Bristol Omnibus Co. This vehicle was then shipped to France, with both BCV and BOC staff in attendance, to spend a fortnight in Gloucester's twin town, Metz, in order to be included in 'British Shopping Week' celebrations. There the bus was continually in use and attracted great interest, despite the French having expected a red rather than green double-decker to appear! It ran faultlessly and operated some 1,500 miles throughout the tour. HHW 933D was then returned to Mansfield by the end of April, but in June it journeyed again to appear at the Essex County Show disguised as an Eastern National bus, before returning once more to Mansfield.

By early 1968 HHW 933D had been renumbered 499 by Mansfield District but again visited Bristol in April, before continuing in the custody of the Mansfield operator where it was to remain – although spending some time out of use – until May 1970. It then came back to Bristol to join GGM 431D which had also returned 'home' during the same month.

Both prototype VRs were then sold by Bristol Commercial Vehicles to the Bristol Omnibus Co to become Nos C5000 and C5001. They

Right:
VRX.002 spent most of its early life allocated to Mansfield District Traction Co and, whilst still green, this involved yet another fleetname change (with BCV legal lettering additionally displayed). Carrying fleet number 555, HHW 933D is here on a crew-operated service to Woodhouse while running for Mansfield District. *BVBG*

were repainted into a new double-deck version of Bristol Omnibus Co's cream and Tilling green OMO livery – since it was intended that they would become the company's first One-Man Operated double-deckers. Unfortunately, agreement was never reached with staff to use these buses without conductors and a series of mechanical problems also caused them to be withdrawn from service for lengthy periods. Indeed, when they were working, it was extremely rare to see them operating all-day services. Generally they appeared on peak-hour schools, works and duplicate journeys from the company's Lawrence Hill depot.

In 1973, both prototypes were sold again, this time to the Essex independent Osborne's of Tollesbury, where they entered operation in a similar livery to that applied by Bristol Omnibus except that the green areas were repainted red. There they stayed together until 1981 when, very regrettably, VRX.002 (HHW 933D) was scrapped, although VRX.001 (GGM 431D) remained with Osborne's for a further six years until its sale, initially to Carter's of Colchester. By this time it had lost its flywheel housing and could not be operated without this vital component to complete the transmission. Valiant efforts were made by Carter's to find a replacement part (which was effectively unique to the prototype VRs), but the task proved impossible, so consideration was given to manufacturing a new component – which itself would have been a daunting task. Nevertheless, with this in mind the bus moved north to another small operator of Bristol vehicles, the Northern Bus Co of Anston, Sheffield. Unfortunately, this meant alternative plans to preserve GGM 431D as a static exhibit were not pursued and very sadly it was eventually sent to a scrap-yard. It had been stripped by the summer of 1991.

Although remaining impressive-looking vehicles throughout their service careers, and whilst retaining enormous design potential, neither of the bodied VR prototypes was to enjoy a reputation for sustained, dependable operation. Indeed, for this reason it is perhaps surprising that they lasted as long as they did. Bristol's reputation as a builder of extremely reliable vehicles was a little tarnished by these buses and it was to be some while before this less-than-desirable image was shaken off by the production VRs that were to follow.

Below left:
In 1970 the VRX prototypes were sold to Bristol Omnibus but spent little time in service. Uniquely, August Bank Holiday Monday 1972 saw them working from Weston-super-Mare to Bristol, where C5001 (HHW 933D) is viewed disgorging passengers. *M. S. Curtis*

Below:
Both prototype VRs moved again during 1973 to Osborne's of Tollesbury, Essex. Now wearing red and cream livery, GGM 431D is seen in wet conditions on the Colchester run, displaying Osborne's fleetname. *The late R. F. Mack*

3

Turning the Engine

Bristol sought to attract customers throughout the bus industry to its longitudinally-engined VRs but, from an early stage, also planned to offer versions with transversely-mounted engines to broaden further the VR's appeal. The company recognised that this not only conformed to the more conventional rear-engined layout already established by Leyland and Daimler but would also permit a reduction in overall vehicle length due to a shorter rear overhang. VRs of similar wheelbase would, nevertheless, be identical forward of the rear axle, regardless of engine position.

Accordingly, further clarification of vehicle types became necessary and Transversely-engined models therefore became known as type VRT while Longitudinally-engined chassis were further redesignated to become type VRL. These designations were then followed by two additional type letters to denote wheelbase and frame height, followed by Bristol's traditional engine code with the number of cylinders and engine manufacturer's initial. For example, a VRT/SL6G indicated a vehicle to be a Vertical Rear Transversely-engined model with Short wheelbase, Low frame and 6-cylinder Gardner engine.

As with the VRL, the VRT was suitable for either double- or single-deck bodywork and was available with wheelbases of either 16ft 2in or 18ft 6in, but the reduced rear overhang produced overall body lengths of 30ft 5in or 32ft 9in respectively. With the option of high or low chassis frames, the complete VRT range comprised VRT/SL, VRT/LL, VRT/SH and VRT/LH models.

The VRT design generated considerable interest following publication of full details in the summer of 1967 as the short wheelbase VRLs were still some 3ft longer than Bristol FLF Lodekkas (or equivalent front-engined buses) which represented the longest double-deckers in many existing fleets. Those who felt the VRL was just a little too long therefore saw the VRT as an acceptable replacement double-deck model. Indeed, such interest was shown in the VRT type, with orders far outweighing those for the VRL, that it was hurriedly placed into production with even less preparation and testing than the longitudinally-engined VR. This was possibly due to a degree of over-confidence on the part of both operators and manufacturer, who believed the more established transverse engine position, coupled to Bristol's almost legendary reputation for relia-

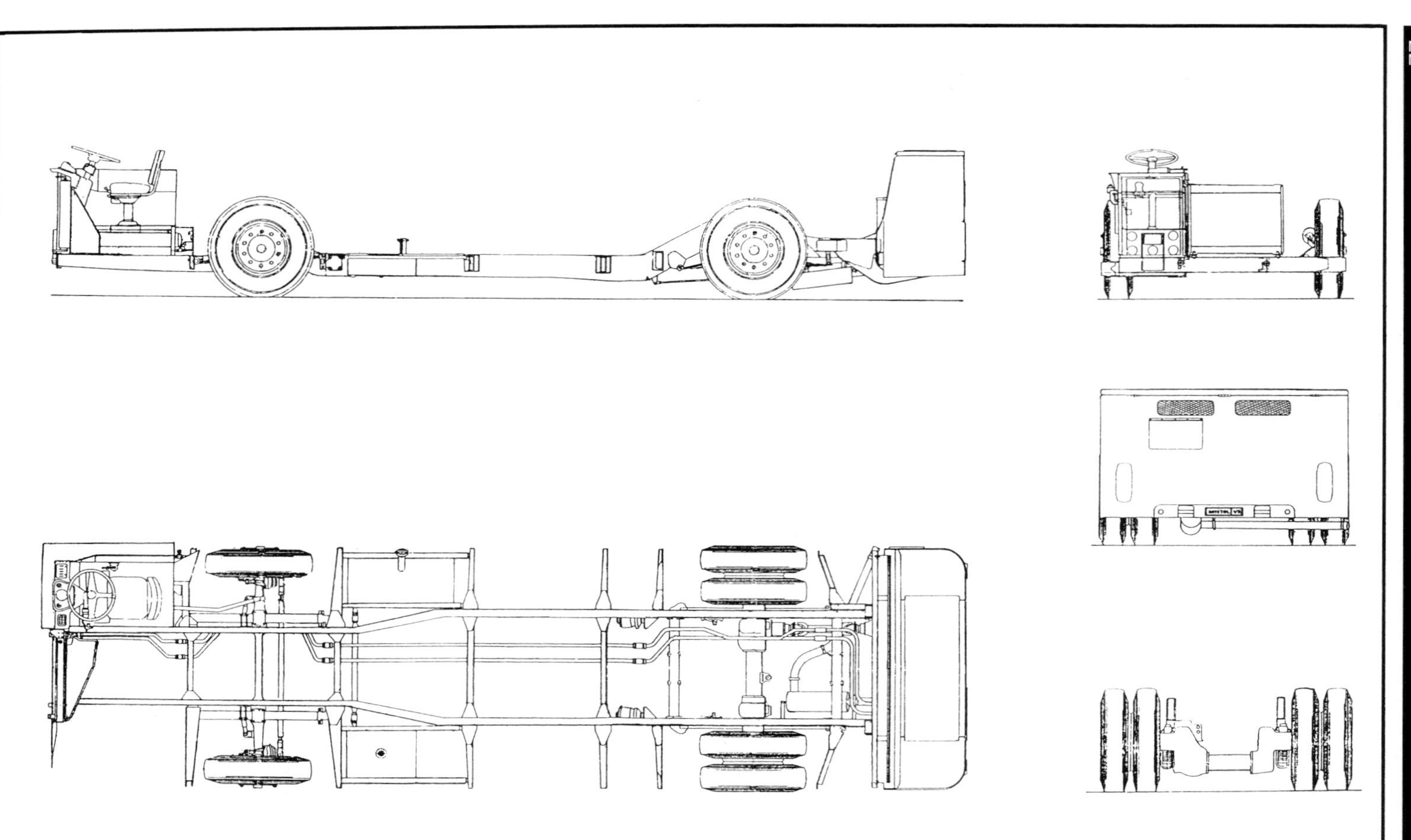

A drawing of an early Bristol type VRT/SL chassis.

bility, would result in a bus of the very best quality. Unfortunately, at first, this was not to be – and it was a mistake which cost Bristol dearly during the initial years of VR production!

Moreover, the desire to rush the VRT into production was accelerated by the introduction of the Government's new bus grant scheme in 1968. This offered operators the opportunity to receive a 25% (and later 50%) grant towards the cost of new buses provided they were suitable for one-man operation and conformed to detailed specifications. Double-deckers with transverse engines such as the Leyland Atlantean, Daimler Fleetline and Bristol VRT complied with these requirements, but the VRL did not, which naturally influenced Bristol customers to buy VRT rather than VRL chassis.

On production Bristol VRs, the cab area was more compact than the VRX prototypes, with a more upright steering column which released more room in the passenger area, while the mechanical handbrake was replaced by an air-operated spring parking brake – Bristol being the first British PSV builder to introduce such a device on production vehicles. Fuel tanks were also relocated from under the driving position to behind the front wheels, but the VRT-version offered rather less scope for locating passenger doors and stairs at the rear than did the VRL design.

VRT engine options included Gardner 6LW, 6LX or 6LXB, or Leyland 0.600 or 0.680 power units, together with a new option – the AEC AV691. Offering up to 205bhp at 2,200rpm, this engine appeared briefly in an attempt to attract AEC customers to the VR, AEC's own rear-engined Routemaster having not entered production following the appearance of a prototype in 1966. Initially, however, only Gardner 6LX or 6LXB engines were ever fitted to early production VRTs.

The VRT's power unit was mounted across the rear, towards the nearside of the vehicle with the gearbox alongside in the rear offside corner of the chassis. The drive was then taken back from the gearbox and turned through mitre spiral bevel gears to the offside of the dropped-centre rear axle, which was identical to the axle used on the VRL. Four- or five-speed gearboxes were offered with semi-automatic or fully automatic control available.

The engine cover of the VRT consisted of a wrap-around glass fibre unit, hinged at the top, which was designed to match the profile of the vehicle body by fitting flush to it, rather than forming a 'bustle' as was usual on other manufacturers' rear-engined double-deckers. This resulted in an extremely unobtrusive arrangement and only the very shallow rear window immediately above the engine caused the power unit's position to be just a little more conspicuous than it was on the VRL. Initially, two small ventilation grilles were included in the rear face of the engine surround, but the urgent need for additional side grilles together with an engine compartment cooling fan was soon realised and these modifications rapidly followed. The design of the engine cover itself was also changed on many VRTs to incorporate two separately-hinged side panels which was more convenient than the bulky one-piece unit originally fitted. As a final touch (which would be noticed by countless following motorists) a 'Bristol VR' badge was attached to the lower edge of the VRT's rear engine cover, in addition to its position on the front of the bus.

ECW's body design for the VRT closely followed the pattern set by the VRX prototypes, although the new engine position necessitated considerable redesign around the rear of the vehicle. In addition to the raised bench seats over the rear wheel arches, an additional bench-seat (for five) was positioned on the same level across the rear of the lower saloon in front of the engine, with the top of the engine compartment behind forming a large parcel shelf. Apart from the raised rear seats, the lower saloon floor of the VRT was otherwise completely flat except for a shallow step near the entrance. The front of the body was almost identical to the longitudinally-engined prototypes, but among minor modifications was the introduction of a large windscreen with central dividing strip rather than two distinctly separate screens.

VRT/LL models carried bodywork broadly comparable with the VRX prototypes of similar length (but with the longer wheelbase in the case of the VRT), while VRT/SL models, with bodywork of just over 30ft length, accommo-

Right:
Bristol hurriedly developed a transverse-engined version of its VR. Here one of the earliest examples is seen while undergoing tests with the company's experimental department. All VRTs were initially Gardner powered, and in this picture, taken from the rear of the chassis, the engine is clearly visibie, coupled to the gearbox on the right via a 17¾in-diameter fluid flywheel. *Bristol*

Centre right:
The first VRTs to be built were 32ft 7in-long VRT/LL models for Scottish Omnibuses of Edinburgh. They were broadly comparable therefore with the two prototype VRXs, although they had a longer wheelbase and, with seating for 83, could accommodate three additional passengers within their ECW bodies. This November 1968 view shows AA286 (LFS 286F) prior to delivery to Scottish Omnibuses, whose vehicles carried the 'Eastern Scottish' name. *ECW*

Bottom right:
The first VRT/SL (with chassis No VRT/SL-101) became Eastern National 3000 (CPU 979G) and is seen during March 1969 departing from Basildon bus station for London King's Cross, shortly after entering service. It is wearing a short-lived Tilling green and cream livery with rather more cream than usual. The chassis of this bus was exhibited on Bristol's stand at the 1968 Commercial Motor Show. *G. R. Mills*

Above:
One of the VRT/SL6Gs diverted from Bristol Omnibus, in this case to Brighton Hove & District, became No 94 (OCD 764G) when finished in BH&D's unique bright red and cream livery. Its ECW bodywork had seating for 70 and, in contrast to the prototype VRXs, the windscreen design of production VRs was changed to include a central metal dividing strip. The grille bar spacing was also slightly revised, resulting in possibly the most overall attractive body design ever to emerge from Lowestoft. *G. R. Mills*

dated around 70-75 passengers depending upon seating pitch and provision for luggage.

With their attractive body lines the ECW-bodied VRs were to develop a classic appearance, which was enhanced further by the addition of Bristol's fibreglass wheel trims on the rear wheels of many VRTs, to become one of the most distinctive double-deckers of the period.

As traditional Bristol customers, it was not surprising that the first VRT orders were placed by the state-owned operators, both in Scotland and south of the border. The first VRTs to be delivered were actually long wheelbase VRT/LL models for Scottish Omnibuses (Eastern Scottish) which ordered 25 such vehicles with 32ft 7in ECW bodywork containing seating for 83 passengers. Registered LFS 280F – LFS 304F, the first of these entered service in November 1968, which in itself was noteworthy since G-suffix registrations had been introduced by this time!

The Scottish Bus Group followed the VRT/LLs with an order for a further 84 VRTs, to VRT/SL specification, as part of its 1969 vehicle replacement programme. Eastern Scottish added 10 of these to the longer VRTs already in service while Central SMT's prototype VRX was joined by 20 VRTs which continued the BN (Bristol N-type) fleet number prefix. The remainder were divided between Alexander (Midland) with 15, and Western SMT with 39 examples, the latter powered by the 10.45-litre Gardner 6LXB 165bhp engine rather than the slightly less powerful 6LX unit. The Alexander (Midland) order was originally intended to receive bodywork by the Scottish bodybuilder, Walter Alexander & Co (Coachbuilders) Ltd, but when delivered all Scottish Bus Group VRTs carried ECW bodywork.

As expected, substantial numbers of VRTs were also produced for the Tilling group which called for 83 VRT/SLs in its orders announced in 1968, all with Eastern Coach Works bodywork naturally. Included among them were 28 for Bristol Omnibus for use on Bristol city routes, and 34 for the West Yorkshire group which included York-West Yorkshire and Keighley-

Above right:
This line-up of 10 dark red Scottish Bus Group VRT/SLs, destined for Central SMT and Western SMT, await modification at Bristol's Bath Road (Top) works before delivery in the summer of 1969. The Western examples seated 75 while those for Central had an even higher capacity of 77.
Bristol

Below right:
A rear view of an early United Auto VRT, No 615 (WHN 815G), showing the very compact engine compartment with cover secured by Triumph Herald-type catches. This bus was among those diverted from Bristol Omnibus, whose Lawrence Hill depot is ironically the location of this April 1969 picture, where modifications were being undertaken to assist BCV.
A. R. Macfarlane

West Yorkshire services. Other early VRT operators among Tilling companies were Thames Valley, United Counties, Western National and Eastern National. Indeed, the first VRT/SL to be built, with chassis No VRT/SL-101, was allocated to Eastern National after display (in chassis form) on Bristol's stand at the 1968 Commercial Motor Show held at Earls Court. It was exhibited alongside an example of Bristol's new lightweight LH-type chassis with horizontal engine mounted amidships, carrying a Plaxton coach body. VRT/SL-101 later received a 70-seat body at Eastern Coach Works to become Eastern National 3000 (CPU 979G).

The order for 28 VRTs for the Bristol fleet had provisionally been placed as early as the summer of 1966 for delivery under the 1967/68 new vehicle programme. An internal memorandum of June 1966 (which still classified these vehicles as N-types) stated that fleet numbers in the 5000 series were to be allocated to them. Unfortunately, Bristol Omnibus later decided to change its new vehicle policy in favour of Bristol RE high capacity single-deckers and so the VRT order was diverted to Brighton Hove & District and United Automobile Services which received eight and 20 respectively of the Bristol allocation.

Nevertheless some of these 28 vehicles were soon to be seen on BOC premises in Bristol as it quickly became apparent that a number of minor modifications to the VRTs were required. These included a change of rear axle ratios for their new customers but, more seriously, the others again reflected the speed with which this model was pressed into production. The magnitude of the problems then became more obvious, for while it was not unusual to see newly-completed vehicles passing through BCV's works for a variety of reasons, the nature of the VRT problems were rather more significant and substantial numbers were to arrive at BCV's Brislington works. Indeed, such was the volume of work required that Bristol Omnibus was asked to assist, undertaking these tasks in their own workshops at Lawrence Hill and Marlborough Street. Among the buses involved was a batch of some 20 VRTs for Central SMT and Western SMT, which arrived in Bristol from ECW in July 1969 – yet the first of these were not seen in Scotland until three months later, when released following modification!

These problems did nothing to impress the Scottish group companies, which never again favoured Bristol with orders for the VR! And if this were not bad enough, there was a serious accident when one of the original VRT/LLs of Eastern Scottish shed a wheel that fatally injured a pedestrian, while a series of engine compartment fires also plagued VRTs with other SBG companies.

The situation with the Tilling VRTs was a little happier, although difficulties arose with the earliest models as the lack of development and testing before the commencement of production once more became plainly evident, with mitre box and fluid flywheel faults being among the causes of transmission failure. The Tilling engineers persevered with the VRT, however, encouraged largely by the potential benefits of one-man operation, with many operators experiencing critical staff shortages.

In 1969, repeat orders were placed by Brighton Hove & District (10), Thames Valley (two), United Automobile (13) and United Counties (15), while other customers to call for VRTs were Eastern Counties (five), Lincolnshire (six), Midland General (two), Southern Vectis (three) and, following its operation of VRX.002, Mansfield District (three).

Bristol also achieved notable success in winning two important orders for VRTs from municipalities, in both cases with bodywork by East Lancashire Coachbuilders Ltd, rather than ECW. The first was for Liverpool Corporation which specified 25 33ft-long VRT/LH chassis with dual entrance/exit bodywork. These featured Gardner 6LXB engines housed in a rear engine bustle similar to that found on Atlanteans and Fleetlines instead of the neat enclosed arrangement favoured by ECW. The first entered service in 1970, by which time Liverpool's buses had become part of the newly-formed Merseyside Passenger Transport Executive (PTE). The second municipal customer was

Right:
The Derbyshire-based Midland General Omnibus Co painted its double-deckers (but not its single-deckers) in a blue livery, relieved by cream window surrounds. Among early VRT/SLs to receive this treatment was its No 316 (BNU 680G), a 70-seat Gardner 6LX-engined bus, seen reversing at Nottingham on route B1 to Ripley.
R. H. G. Simpson

Below right:
Another Scottish VRT/SL6G, this time in the blue and cream livery of W. Alexander & Sons (Midland) Ltd. New in 1970, it is seen entering Falkirk bus station carrying fleet No MRT 15 (SMS 45H). Its ECW bodywork seats 77, has shallow hopper window vents and yet another side/indicator light arrangement. *S. J. Brown*

Stockport which, like Liverpool, was to become part of a PTE, in this case South-East Lancashire & North-East Cheshire (SELNEC). Ten Stockport VRs were built to VRT/SL specification with Gardner 6LX engines but, during the course of their bodying, a disastrous fire at East Lancs' factory destroyed or badly damaged the whole batch (together with one of the VRT/LHs intended for Merseyside). As a result, the entire Stockport order was lost, but one chassis was salvaged and three years later emerged in Australia with Hill's Bus Service of Wollongong, carrying a 47-seat Smithfield single-deck body! Of course both VRT and VRL chassis were designed for either double- or single-deck coachwork, but Hill's VRT was to be the only Bristol VR ever to receive a single-deck body.

Despite early difficulties with the VRT design, Bristol rapidly improved the reliability of this model to increase substantially its following (outside Scotland!). By the end of 1970, 287 examples of the initial version had been built, and preparations had been made for the introduction of an improved VRT which would restore much of the lost confidence in the company's rear-engined double-decker.

Right:
Merseyside PTE, having absorbed Liverpool Corporation's buses, became the only purchaser of the Bristol VRT/LH model. Among those originally ordered by Liverpool was No 2041 (UKD 535H), viewed here in Derby Square, Liverpool. Delivered in 1970, these vehicles had 80-seat, dual-door bodywork with high floors built by East Lancs, finished in Liverpool green but carrying the new PTE insignia.
M. S. Curtis

Below right:
The only single-deck Bristol VR ever built was based on chassis No VRT/SL-332. This chassis was among those originally ordered by Stockport Corporation and involved in the 1970 East Lancs factory fire, but while all the others were destroyed, this one was salvaged and three years later emerged in Australia with Hill's Bus Service! Carrying a 47-seat Smithfield body, and appearing rather longer than a standard VRT/SL, it received licence No M/O 6219 and is captured here loading for Hill's home town of Wollongong.
L. J. Pascoe

4

Production VRLs

Despite the introduction of the VRT chassis, Bristol persevered with the VRL design with its simpler drive-line which continued to attract considerable interest, particularly for applications where the bus grant scheme would not apply. The VRL was therefore produced in parallel to the VRT and the potential versatility of the VRL design was not entirely lost, even though longitudinally-engined vehicles were to be totally excluded from the bus grant specifications. However, the attraction of having part of the cost of new buses met by Government was too much for most bus operators to resist and, given the choice, they opted for a vehicle such as the VRT which qualified for the grant.

Nevertheless, there was a role for the VRL and the first production examples were assembled late in 1967. They differed in a number of respects from the earlier prototypes, which had been described as VRL 'Series 1s', but production VRLs did not automatically assume the title 'Series 2'. This term was applied to later VRL chassis which incorporated further improvements.

The changes from late 1967 brought the area forward of the rear axle into line with that proposed for the VRT, with the introduction of a shorter cab and spring parking brake as standard. Gone too was the under-cab fuel tank, replaced by tanks of 40-gallon capacity behind the front wheels. Wheelbases remained at 16ft 2in or 18ft 6in with frame heights of 18in or 21in but details at the front of the chassis, including around the radiator, were among other modifications. With equivalent chassis variants to the VRT, the VRL range comprised four versions, namely: VRL/SL, VRL/LL, VRL/SH and VRL/LH types. Gardner and Leyland engine options, similar to those of the transversely-engined chassis, were also listed, but variety among production VRLs was to be extremely limited as only VRL/LH chassis with Leyland 0.680 power units were specified by any of the three customers that were to order the Bristol VRL.

The first production VRL, with chassis No VRL/LH-101, was also the first Bristol chassis to be exported following the lifting of sales restrictions, and was destined for a customer in South Africa. This gave BCV a particularly significant boost as batches of Bristol LWL types for South Africa were among the last chassis shipped abroad before nationalisation halted exports. Bristol could therefore demonstrate that it was literally capturing orders where they had been left some 20 years earlier! The VRL's new customer was the Municipality of Johannesburg, and the first chassis was the forerunner of a series which was delivered in completely knocked down (ckd) condition for assembly locally. Chassis No 101 was assembled by Bristol to act as a pattern for the others, and was shipped from Southampton Docks in November 1967.

On arrival in South Africa, chassis 101 received locally-built bodywork by Bus Bodies (South Africa) Ltd of Port Elizabeth. This

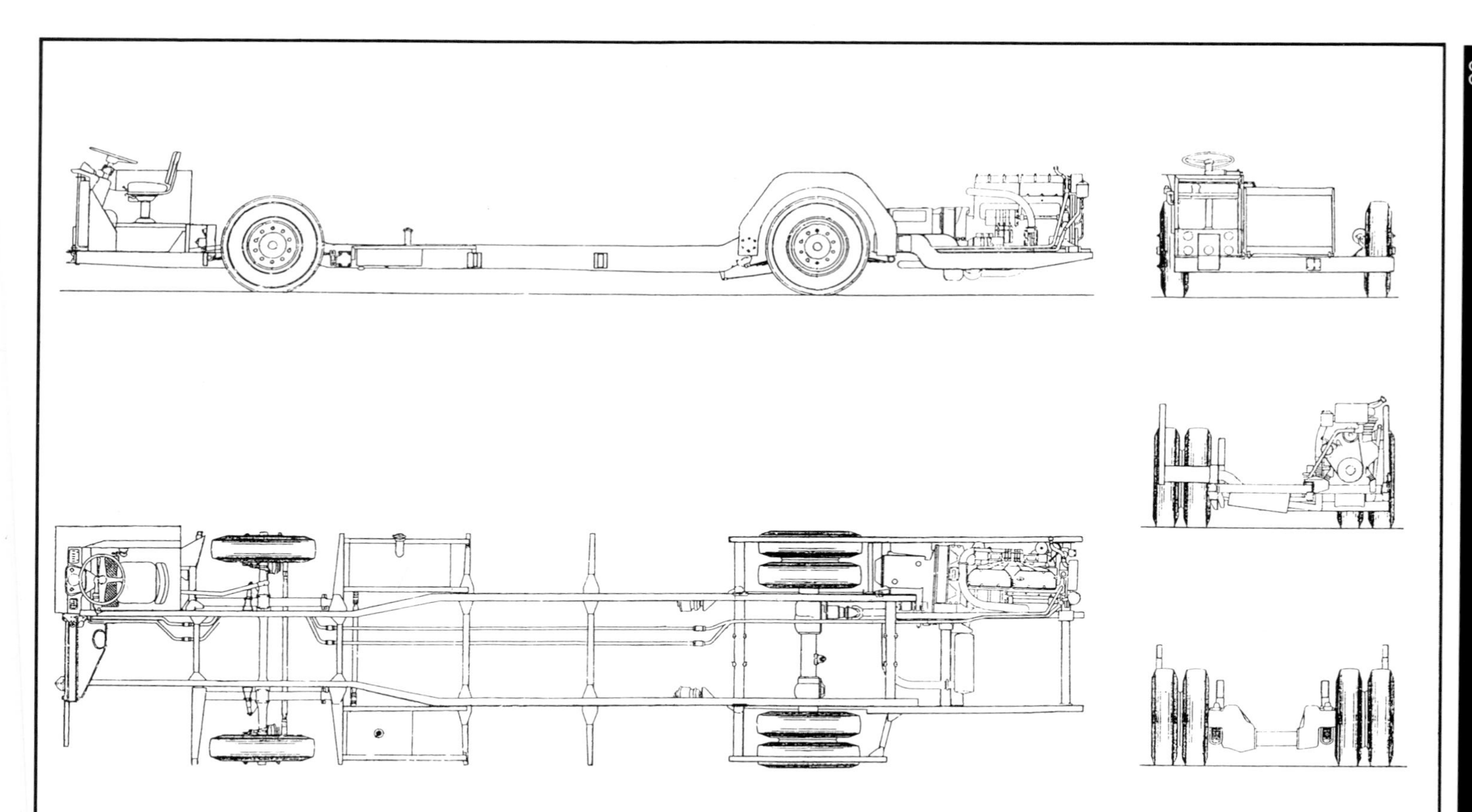

A drawing of a Bristol VRL/LH chassis.

exploited fully the potential of the VRL chassis layout for, although it was claimed to be suitable for one-man operation, it carried dual-door bodywork. It had a passenger entrance door at the front (opposite the driver's cab) and an exit behind the back axle at the extreme rear – in a similar position to that found on traditional, front-engined double-deckers. Two staircases were also included, behind the cab and at the extreme rear, while seating was available for 85 passengers within the 36ft long body, with provision for a further 15 standees. Fully automatic Bristol/SCG transmissions and power-assisted steering completed the specification, and the first example in the Johannesburg fleet (which became fleet No 317) was followed by a further 13 similar VRLs.

The second production VRL/LH (chassis No 102) was for a British customer. It was the first of what became among the most impressive coaches ever seen on British roads and motorways, and which were arguably at least a decade ahead of their time. The buyer for this chassis was Ribble's coaching subsidiary, W.C. Standerwick Ltd, and the vehicle – which was heralded as Britain's largest coach – carried an experimental ECW 36ft-long double-deck coach body with seating for 60 passengers together with an enormous luggage compartment and on-board toilet facilities. It was built with the close co-operation of the

Right:
FCK 450G (fleet No 50 S) was the first of the impressive VRL/LH6L coaches for Ribble's subsidiary, W. C. Standerwick Ltd. At the time it was posing for ECW's official photographer in September 1968, it was the largest coach in Britain. In addition to seating for 60 passengers in considerable comfort, a toilet compartment and huge rear luggage area were contained within its coachwork, which was finished in Standerwick's smart dark red and cream livery. *ECW*

Below right:
The 36ft long single-deckers were only just gaining widespread acceptance in the late 1960s so the sheer size of a double-decker built to this length made a colossal impact. Accordingly, FCK 450G caused many heads to turn when exhibited at the 1968 Commercial Motor Show and later on entry into service. With the panelled lower rear section of the body, the engine position was even less obvious on VRL coaches, although additional engine cooling grilles were found to be desirable as operational experience was gained. *ECW*

Right:
Among the distinctive features of all ECW bodies for VRL coaches were wrap-around screens on both decks, as displayed here by Standerwick No 69 (OCK 69K), one of the 1971 batch of VRL coaches. Modifications were made to the design following experience with FCK 450G, including the repositioning of the offside emergency exit to behind the front axle, the provision of a cooling grille on the side of the engine cover (which in this case has an additional scoop to improve inward air flow), while the use of polished wheel trims was abandoned. *G. Coxon*

operator for use on express services between London and the Northwest, and was designed for cruising at up to 70mph, which at the time represented a high speed for any coach, especially a double-decker! Registered FCK 450G (fleet No 50.S), it appeared at Earls Court in September 1968 on ECW's stand where it was one of the outstanding exhibits of that year's Commercial Motor Show.

Once again the VRL layout allowed considerable freedom when designing the body. While there was a hinged door opposite the driver, the main passenger door was in the centre, while stairs were located over the rear axle. The toilet compartment was situated alongside the stairs while the luggage area was reached through a full height door at the rear of the coach. Forced-air ventilation was offered to all 42 top-deck passengers (supplemented by roof vents), while sliding windows provided supplementary ventilation for the 18 lower deck passengers. The driver was not overlooked either, with five-speed epicyclic transmission and power-assisted steering producing reduced levels of fatigue.

Extensive testing of this vehicle was followed by its maiden run from Blackpool to London in December 1968. It was followed by further batches of similar vehicles which replaced Ribble's ageing Leyland Atlantean 'Gay Hostess' double-deckers. The VRLs rapidly earned a reputation for speed and comfort, although occasional mechanical problems, usually associated with the driveline, did cause complications.

Eleven further VRL coaches were ordered by Ribble for 1970 delivery and they, like the original vehicle, were finished in Standerwick's attractive cream and dark red livery. A number of minor modifications were made, including enlargement of the engine cooling grilles and the positioning of both fuel tanks and filler neck on the nearside, while the fitting of polished wheel discs was abandoned. The body was also slightly revised with the removal of the frosted-glass window in the rear luggage compartment door, while the offside emergency exit was moved forward to a position behind the front axle, which unfortunately spoilt the lower-deck window pillar spacing just a little.

This batch was numbered 51-61 (LRN 51 – LRN 61J) and the first entered service in November 1970. Their performance – together with that of the original VRL coach – was nothing short of breathtaking. The ride was smooth yet there was no shortage of power. When one remembers many family saloon cars at that time were still not built to cruise on motorways at speeds as high as 70mph, it is not difficult to understand why many motorists displayed amazement as a VRL raced past them with such apparent ease! Yet despite ample power (the Leyland 0.680 unit developed 175bhp at 2,000rpm), there was virtually no engine noise in either saloon – and when idling only the gentle swaying of the vehicle or occasional glimpse of exhaust fumes gave any clue that the engine was running. With excellent forward visibility, passengers were most comfortable in these impressive coaches, although for drivers the difficulty in hearing the engine did not assist in timing gear changes.

Meanwhile, VRLs continued to enjoy success in South Africa with an order for a further 11 VRL/LH6L buses received from Pretoria City Transport. In most respects these were similar to those for Johannesburg and again were bodied in Port Elizabeth by Bus Bodies (SA) with twin staircases and dual doors, but in this case seating was reduced to only 82 as a stand and counter were provided over the rear nearside wheel-arch where a conductor was to be located.

A little further south, the Johannesburg VRLs were joined by a number of Daimler CRC6-36 models. These were basically Daimler Fleetlines but with the engine fitted longitudinally in VRL fashion (and carrying 36ft-long bodies like those fitted to the Bristols). In fact, Daimler displayed such a vehicle at the 1968 Commercial Motor Show intended for use in Walsall, but in view of the limited opportunities for such a chassis in Britain following the introduction of bus grants, Daimler hurriedly withdrew this design of double-decker. Indeed, it was slightly ironic that after successfully producing its Fleetline, Daimler considered it necessary to try for itself the VRL layout while Bristol, with its VRT, was doing the reverse! It is also interesting that the Daimler vehicles employed Cummins Vee engines, as similar power units were later tried in South African Bristol VRLs since they were believed to be more suitable for the prevailing climatic conditions.

Right:
A rear view of another of the VRL coaches, this time No 65 photographed in Birmingham *en route* to London. It illustrates further modifications to the original VRL coach design, the most obvious being the enlarged engine cooling grilles and an unglazed rear luggage compartment door, while the nearside filler cap shows the revised positioning of the fuel tanks.
B. L. Thompson

Below right:
No 78 (PRN 78K), the penultimate VRL coach, was completed in the summer of 1972 at the time when white National coach livery was being introduced for NBC companies. However, rather surprisingly, No 78 was finished in a non-standard livery of white with 'National' and small 'Standerwick' fleetnames, but with light blue window surrounds and skirt.
V. H. Darling

Right:
The last VRL coach, No 79 was completed in July 1972 and was finished in all-over white 'National' coach livery. Eventually the entire fleet of Standerwick VRLs was repainted in this style, which was far less flattering than a two-colour scheme. This late evening scene at London's Victoria coach station in September 1974 shows No 52 (LRN 52J) resting before its return journey north. A small Standerwick name was retained towards the front of these coaches, but ownership of the VRLs had discreetly passed to National Travel (North West) by this date. *M. S. Curtis*

Below:
Six of the VRL coaches were sold to Tyne & Wear PTE in 1976 for use on Scandinavian ferry transfer services to the Tyne Commission Quay, and although repainted in Tyne & Wear yellow and cream livery, they were actually operated on behalf of the PTE by Northern General. Now numbered 37, OCK 67K awaits its next load at Newcastle Central station in this July 1981 photograph. *M. S. Curtis*

On the home market, Ribble announced an order for an additional 18 VRL double-deck coaches during the summer of 1970, 10 of which were for delivery the next year with the final eight scheduled for 1972 arrival. All were similar in appearance to the first batch except for the last two vehicles, which were built in the summer of 1972 and appeared in revised liveries. By this time the National Bus Company (of which Ribble-Standerwick was part) had decreed that the coaches of its subsidiaries should be repainted in a new white livery with 'National' fleetnames, rather than the colours of individual companies. Consequently, the penultimate VRL (No 78) was finished in white (but with light blue window surrounds) while the last of the batch (No 79) was delivered in all-over white. The latter version was eventually adopted as standard for all 30 of the Standerwick VRLs, which was far less flattering than the original cream and dark red scheme, while No 79 was also to be the last VRL ever built, bringing to an end Bristol's original N-type concept with rear, longitudinally-mounted engine.

The 30 Standerwick coaches established themselves on express services between London and the Northwest over a number of years but, despite some redesign work, they developed a reputation for being prone to differential and gearbox failures. However, in the early hours of 26 July 1974, disaster struck. On that occasion one of the VRLs was travelling south on the M1 motorway near Luton when, while overtaking a line of lorries, the driver encountered a lamp standard across the lane in front of him, which was the result of a lorry having 'jack-knifed' moments before.

Above right:
When withdrawn from long-distance express coach duties, several of the VRLs moved to London sightseeing work. Finished here in plain red, LRN 56J waits at Grosvenor Gardens, Victoria in April 1977, while on hire to London Transport for operation on LT's Round London Sightseeing Tour. It was owned at this time by Destination London. *M. S. Curtis*

Right:
Chassis No VRL/LH-101 was the first of 14 similar chassis for Johannesburg, and upon completion in November 1967 was shipped from Southampton to South Africa, where it received bodywork at Port Elizabeth. The following chassis were shipped in ckd condition for local assembly. *Bristol*

Above:
This is one of the Johannesburg VRL/LH6Ls shortly after completion of its 85-seat bodywork by Bus Bodies (South Africa) Ltd (Busaf). This body design took full advantage of the VRL's layout with passenger doors at the extreme front and rear, and staircases located behind the cab and on the rear platform. There is no doubt that the concept of the Bristol VRL chassis — which permitted such an arrangement — was ingenious, and it remains a matter of regret that the longitudinally-engined VR was never allowed to develop fully. *Busaf*

Right:
An interior view of the rear lower deck of a Johannesburg VRL with the engine position so well disguised that it is easy to mistake this for a traditional front-engined, rear-entrance double-decker. With the staircase rising from the rear platform and inward-facing bench seats over the rear wheels, an interesting comparison is provided with the interior rear of the original VRX prototype vehicles (see page 17). *Busaf*

Right:
Pretoria ordered 11 VRL/LHs, one of which is viewed here outside the Busaf coachworks at Port Elizabeth. It is finished in primer in readiness for the application of an overall advertisement, which was a popular alternative to fleet livery for Pretoria buses. Unlike those for Johannesburg (which were suitable for one-man operation), the Pretoria VRLs were crew operated with a conductor positioned over the nearside rear wheel, hence the absence of glazing in this position. *Busaf*

The driver swerved to avoid a collision but, after several skids, the coach eventually toppled over. Three passengers died and 39 were injured, some seriously.

Coach safety on motorways has frequently been an emotive subject, and this incident (which received national press and TV coverage) added further to the debate. Within days some senior politicians were calling for a total ban on double-deckers from motorways. Although this has never happened, National Travel, which had assumed control of the vehicles from Ribble, decided to withdraw prematurely the VRL coaches from April 1976, following further questions in Parliament and requests for consideration to be given to speed and lane restrictions for double-deckers as measures designed to improve coach safety.

There was no shortage of buyers eager to obtain the VRLs, however, and the first vehicle sold, FCK 450G, was acquired by Coastal Coaches of Newhaven. Tyne & Wear PTE bought six for use between Newcastle Central station and the Tyne Commission Quay where the VRLs' huge luggage compartment was extremely useful. A number of others were employed on sightseeing work, particularly in London, while elsewhere in the country many operators were anxious to obtain a VRL coach as they were perceived as prestigious 'flagships' for smaller independent fleets. Accordingly, among other new liveries applied to VRL coaches were those of CK of Cardiff, Eagle of Bristol, Ementon (European Travel) Cranfield, International Coach Lines, Stagecoach of Perth and Thomas Cook. Some examples also found their way abroad with several exported to Australia and the United States, one of which was still operating in Chicago in the late 1980s, fitted with bus-type rather than coach seats.

Restrictions on double-deck coach operations never were introduced and, a decade after the last VRL was built, a new generation of double-deck coaches appeared, including examples built by Bristol and ECW. And whilst the VRL underwent less development and enjoyed a shorter production run than it deserved, at least one application – the VRL/LH motorway coach – set standards that would be revived in years to follow.

Bristol may have preferred the VRL concept to that of the VRT, and may have wished to develop the rear longitudinally-engined chassis still further, but the lack of demand because it did not attract bus grants meant that legislation effectively killed off this outstandingly versatile design. With only 55 production VRLs constructed, it would be left to the VRT to continue Bristol's rear-engined double-deck development.

Above:
Two Bristol VRL/LHs in service with Pretoria City Transport, that nearest the camera numbered 810 (TP 114. 144), both wearing advertising liveries. Johannesburg VRLs displayed standard 'Bristol VR' badges but it will be noticed that those in Pretoria carried 'Leyland' lettering — which was the source of some annoyance for many in Bristol!
S. J. Brown

Below:
Pretoria 811 (TP 109. 645) stands at Church Square, Pretoria on route 20. A mixture of deep sliding windows and inward-opening vents was fitted to the bodies of Pretoria's VRLs, representing another variation from the Johannesburg examples which had only inward-opening windows.
S. J. Brown

5

Series Two VRTs and NBC

During 1970, Bristol introduced an improved version of its VRT model, the VRT Series 2, which incorporated further improvements and modifications to overcome the initial teething troubles experienced with early production models. In doing so it helped restore Bristol's reputation for producing reliable and well-designed vehicles.

When viewing a VRT Series 2 on the road there was little visible evidence of the changes, and those with ECW bodywork were almost identical to earlier VRT buses. The engine surround had however been standardised on a design incorporating hinged side sections with a lift-up centre panel at the rear, while a very minor change by ECW was the repositioning of the rear offside drainage slot (on the waistband) to a point ahead of, rather than just behind, the rear wheels.

Sets of shallow sliding or hopper window ventilators also disappeared from ECW's VR bodywork, replaced by the deeper versions of Widney 'ECW Slide-a-Lite' slider and hopper vents, arranged alternately. These had already been adopted by the ex-Tilling companies, and henceforth were to become standard fittings.

The VRT/SH variant, which had never been produced, was dropped from this time, leaving three VRT chassis types, whilst the overall length of chassis 'officially' grew by 2¾in owing to a slightly longer rear overhang. Engine options were reduced to simply Gardner's 6LX or 6LXB, or Leyland's 0.680 unit, although only Gardner engines continued to be specified by VRT customers, while four- or five-speed gearboxes remained available with leaf suspension as standard. Perhaps of greater importance was that the Series 2 VRT benefited from the gradual improvements to the transmission and drive, reducing many of the problems that had afflicted the earliest VRTs.

The first three VRT Series 2 chassis (chassis Nos VRT/SL-2-101/102/103) were ordered originally by Southern Vectis but, significantly, were diverted to the former British Electric Traction group company, City of Oxford Motor Services. This reflected the influence of the newly-formed National Bus Company (NBC) which, from 1 January 1969, assumed control of not only the former Tilling fleets but also the ex-BET group companies – which had sold out to the State the previous year. One consequence of this shift in ownership was that many of the traditional boundaries and territories of NBC group companies were progressively modified, with many of the smaller fleets being placed under the control of neighbouring operators, often resulting in the merger of

Right:
A new chassis numbering series commenced for Series 2 VRT/SLs, with VRT/SL-2-101 becoming Oxford 901 (OFC 901H), the first of a trio of VRT/SL6Gs ordered by Southern Vectis but diverted by NBC to City of Oxford Motor Services. Viewed when brand-new in 1970, it is painted in a simplified version of the company's dark red and duck egg green. The only certain method of identifying a Series 2 VRT with ECW body is by the rearmost offside drainage slot on the waistband, which had moved forward compared with earlier VRTs! *G. R. Mills*

Centre right:
Among the most attractive colour schemes ever applied to passenger vehicles must be Southdown's classic apple green and cream, with dark green trim. Although traditionally a Leyland user from the former BET group, significant numbers of VRTs appeared with this company from 1970. Here newly-completed Southdown 519 (WCD 519K) stands outside ECW's Lowestoft coachworks (alongside a Standerwick VRL) in September 1971, just before delivery. *P. Gascoine*

Bottom right:
Another former BET operator was Devon General, whose No 550 (VOD 550K) is seen at Exeter bus station in August 1971, a few days after entering service. Finished in cherry red and ivory, notable features include a one-piece destination display and rear wheel discs, while power was provided by a Gardner 6LX engine. *C. L. Caddy*

Right:
An upper-deck interior view of sister vehicle VOD 549K, typifying the top-deck layout of hundreds of VRs, with seating for 39. In this case Western National group influence is apparent with seats upholstered in Holdsworth's Tilling-style moquette. *M. S. Curtis*

fleets from the previously rival BET and THC organisations.

The National Bus Company also inherited the former THC interests in bus manufacturing at Bristol and Lowestoft, but these were reduced to 50% as the British Leyland Motor Corporation (as it had become) increased its share to 50%. Accordingly, NBC and British Leyland became equal partners with neither having overall control of Bristol or ECW, but Leyland assumed day-to-day responsibility for the works and it became increasingly apparent that Leyland influence would eventually dominate the Bristol factories.

At this point it is appropriate to mention the very high degree of loyalty that existed among the entire Bristol work-force, which was quite exceptional and the envy of many other vehicle builders. Such was the pride which had been established over many years that, initially, there was disbelief that design flaws should have been associated with the earliest VRs. It became of major importance to correct these faults, not least to enable the workforce to again believe that each chassis driven from the works was destined for a long service life – its reputation resting on the Bristol name it carried. Staff attributed some of the failures to Leyland's involvement, but this was never allowed to compromise the high quality of either individual components or the final vehicle assembly.

The National Bus Company meanwhile had the task of integrating two formerly opposing groups of operators, and while the Tilling companies had long been traditional Bristol/ECW customers, Bristol was given the opportunity to penetrate the former BET companies (some having already purchased Bristol RE single-deckers) since any resistance to buying Bristol models in this sector had now been completely removed.

A total of 129 VRTs were ordered by the NBC in 1970 and examples began to appear in the liveries of such famous former BET companies as Southdown (which had taken control of Brighton Hove & District), Ribble, Devon General and East Midland (which would assume responsibility for Mansfield District), in addition to many of the traditional former Tilling group customers.

Further evidence of Tilling/BET integration could also be found at the 1970 Commercial Motor Show. Only one Bristol VR was exhibited, a standard 70-seat bus-bodied version for York-West Yorkshire (YVR55; FWT 955J) displayed on Eastern Coach Works' stand. However, alongside was an ECW LH single-deck bus body incorporating a wrap-around front and BET style curved windscreen rather than the Tilling-style flat windscreen. An ECW-bodied RELL single-decker on Bristol's own stand also carried a similar curved windscreen, which had been established by the BET group over some years as it deflected internal reflections (which could impair a driver's vision at night) far better than flat glass. Its use by ECW therefore clearly illustrated how the vehicle policies of the former Tilling and BET concerns were moving closer together, although for the

Right:
The first Northern Counties-bodied Bristol VRs, and the first VRT/SLs to enter service carrying bodywork other than by ECW, joined Gelligaer UDC during April 1971. Having become so familiar with coachwork by ECW, the body design of these vehicles appeared unnecessarily severe in comparison. These buses were also noteworthy in becoming the nearest operational VRs to Bristol's factory, when new. No 41 (BTX 541J), one of three such vehicles, leaves Newport (then in Monmouthshire) during June 1971. *M. S. Curtis*

time being flat glass continued to be used for VRT windscreens.

The 1970 Commercial Motor Show also saw the début of the integral Leyland National single-deck bus, which entered production 18 months later in a purpose-built factory at Workington. Like Bristol and ECW, the Leyland National Co Ltd was jointly owned by British Leyland and NBC on a 50/50 basis, and it soon became obvious that NBC operating companies were under some pressure to purchase this model in preference to Bristol's RE single-decker. Accordingly, there was considerable concern at both Bristol and Lowestoft that the introduction of the Leyland National would seriously reduce demand for Bristol/ECW products. However it so happened that after a period when one-man operated single-deckers had increased in popularity, operators were returning once more to double-deckers, especially for urban operations, which fortunately allowed Bristol and ECW to continue at full capacity. Moreover, NBC had decided to standardise on the Bristol/ECW VRT as its main double-deck model and, in 1972, when NBC announced its orders for the following year, no fewer than 249 VRTs were called for (all with ECW bodywork) – and the VR was the only double-deck type required, rather than a mix of VRT, Atlantean and Fleetline as on previous occasions. This brought further ex-BET companies into the ranks of VRT operators including East Yorkshire, Yorkshire Traction, Maidstone & District, Trent, Northern General and Potteries Motor Traction.

By then, Bristol Omnibus had at last received its first new Bristol VRs, eight ECW-bodied VRT/SLs (with 180bhp 6LXB engines and four-speed semi-automatic gearboxes) having arrived for Bristol City Services in February 1972, although these did not enter regular service until July of that year owing to a delay in reaching agreement with operating staff over the use of these vehicles without conductors. It was fashionable during this period for many one-man operated buses, especially for use in cities or towns, to have bodywork featuring a separate front entrance and centre exit, which was designed to speed passenger boarding and alighting times. The 70-seat Bristol Omnibus VRTs, together with a batch of similar buses built at the same time for Southdown, were the first ECW-bodied VRTs constructed to this layout. While ECW maintained a reputation for high quality and well thought-out bodywork, the design of its two-door VRT body fell short of the high standards normally achieved.

Externally, the attractive appearance was retained but inside it was a different story. The centre exit was positioned two bays behind the front axle with the staircase immediately

Above:
The merger of Aldershot & District with Thames Valley at the beginning of 1972 resulted in the appearance of a new fleetname — Alder Valley. A new dark red livery was also introduced but this was short-lived because of the adoption of NBC's standard colour schemes later the same year. Here Bristol VRT/SL6G No 920 (FBL 112K) displays the inaugural Alder Valley image upon formation of the new company. *Alder Valley*

Below:
While Alder Valley succeeded Thames Valley as provider of inter-urban services from Reading, the local municipal operator, Reading Transport, was introducing its own Bristol VRs on the town's bus network. These were Gardner 6LX-engined, long-wheelbase VRT/LL models with Northern Counties dual-door centre-staircase bodywork. With capacity for over 90 passengers, they were promoted locally as 'Jumbos', as demonstrated by No 28 (XRD 28K). *Reading Transport*

opposite, rather than over the front wheel arch. As a result, the centre doors and stairs caused the removal of several pairs of forward facing seats while the number of high-mounted bench seats was increased, with these positioned over each wheel arch and another across the rear of the saloon. Consequently, of the 27 passenger seats on the lower deck only 10 were conventionally placed facing forward at floor level, the remaining 17 being mounted on footstools – and 12 of these were side-facing. The stairs turned sharply around 180° within the space of one standard 4ft 3in-long ECW bay, which was far from ideal for a vehicle which should have sought to improve ease of use by passengers. In the upper saloon, 43 seats were accommodated. Here too the door gear covers, especially in the centre, intruded into the passenger area, severely reducing passenger leg-room in these positions. The whole layout was therefore in marked contrast to the spacious and comfortable arrangement of the standard, one-door Eastern Coach Works VRT body.

ECW was not the only bodybuilder for the Series 2 VRT, as another batch of 35 VRT/LHs with East Lancs coachwork was delivered to Merseyside PTE in 1971. In addition, the first Northern Counties bodies for VRTs appeared when three VRT/SL6Gs entered service with the Welsh municipality, Gelligaer UDC. These

Right:
Operation of Bristol VRTs by Bristol Omnibus was not achieved until 1972, when eight 70-seat examples, which were among the first with ECW dual-door bodywork, commenced work. Although delivered in February 1972, they did not begin regular service until 23 July when, supplemented by REs, they converted city services 22/23 to one-man operation. Fleet numbers followed the VRX prototypes and the first of the batch, C5002 (EHU 361K), is seen on the first day at Lockleaze. *M. S. Curtis*

Below right:
Livery for the Bristol Omnibus VRs consisted of standard Tilling green and cream (with Bristol scroll fleetnames) but applied in this style to denote that such buses were one-man operated. This rear offside picture, taken in Marlborough Street, Bristol, illustrates the final member of the original batch of eight, No C5009 (EHU 368K), while working on service 23. It demonstrates how the centre staircase position of these vehicles altered the offside lower-deck window arrangement.
M. S. Curtis

Right:
In 1972 Sheffield Corporation took delivery of 18 VRT/SL6Gs with 73-seat East Lancs bodywork, incorporating an engine bustle. No 269 (OWE 269K) is depicted on service 73. From April 1974 the Sheffield Transport fleet became part of the South Yorkshire PTE and no further VRs were ordered.
R. H. G. Simpson

Below right:
More East Lancs-bodied Bristol VRs appeared in Liverpool with Merseyside PTE from late 1974. Unlike earlier Merseyside examples, they were based on VRT/SL chassis. Finished in the then-new light green and cream livery, No 2118 loads for Garston in Liverpool's James Street. Although of similar style to the Sheffield VRTs, these two body designs shared surprisingly few common parts.
M. S. Curtis

had 77-seat single-door bodies which, whilst of Northern Counties' sound construction, lacked ECW's attractive styling, with the front grille treatment in particular, being quite severe.

ECW's own front end styling for the VRT was about to change, too, as the BET-design curved windscreen (already seen on REs and LHs) was included in the Lowestoft-built double-decker from the summer of 1972 to coincide with the introduction of the 'L' registration mark suffix. A mock-up of the new frontal design had actually been completed 12 months earlier. Simultaneously, the front dash became of a wrap-around design to match the screen while the waistband across the front of the body was reduced in depth. Above the windscreen, the traditional ECW-look was retained but the width of the forward portion of the body was slightly increased, dispensing with the inward tapering design of the original flat front VR body. The basic grille shape (with Bristol and ECW badges) and headlight surround remained, demonstrating how successfully Tilling and BET influence could be combined.

Following the introduction of ECW's revised frontal design came, for the first time, a number of 13ft 5in (rather than 13ft 8in) tall VRTs which were specified by operators requiring an ultra-lowheight double-decker. These could be distinguished by their lack of a waistband over the windscreen together with a slightly sunken gangway in the lower saloon (reminiscent of early Bristol Lodekkas).

Right:
This is Eastern Coach Works on 17 August 1971, giving a foretaste of future VR body production with a green mock-up of a VR front incorporating the curved BET-style windscreen. It was to be a full 12 months before curved-screen VRTs entered production, by which time the skirt below the grille had been reduced in depth to improve ground clearance, and the grille mesh (which here follows the pattern of flat-front VRTs) had also been redesigned. (The number plate carried by the mock-up is believed to have been taken from a Cumberland LH, having become surplus when the latter was re-registered with a later year suffix before display at the 1970 Commercial Motor Show.) *M. S. Curtis*

At the 1972 Commercial Motor Show no fewer than four Bristol VRs appeared, the highest number ever to be displayed at such an exhibition. On Bristol's stand in chassis form was VRT/SL6G No 2-444, which carried both 'Bristol VR' and 'Leyland roundel' badges for the occasion. When bodied, it became C5010 (LHW 791L), the first of a further 20 two-door vehicles for Bristol city routes. This chassis was exhibited alongside an LHL-type which later received coachwork by Plaxtons.

A VR and LH were also displayed on ECW's stand at the same show, both carrying stage carriage bus bodywork. The VR was registered XDL 377L and was destined for Southern Vectis while the LH was intended for Eastern Counties. Significantly, these two buses carried the proposed NBC standard liveries which would soon appear all over England and Wales, as the National Bus Company, having already introduced an overall white livery for its coaches, decided to extend its corporate image to service buses. Originally, several basic colours were expected to be used throughout the group with standard fleetname styles and the National double-N symbol, but this was reduced to either leaf green or poppy red in the vast majority of cases. A handful of companies were permitted to use blue for a short time, but there were very few other exceptions to the strict corporate livery policy.

Naturally, as the new liveries were gradually introduced, many splendid and varied colour schemes – many of which had been long associated with operators in particular areas – were swept aside, which did nothing to improve local goodwill. Moreover, the particular shades of red and green initially used were, in many cases, of appalling quality, which resulted in rapid fading and highlighted the adoption of a poorer image when compared with most of the liveries which had been lost. The show buses on ECW's stand also had seats finished in a mainly blue and red moquette incorporating the NBC logo, but very few vehicles subsequently received this material.

All buses in NBC fleets henceforth appeared in the new standard colours and consequently very few ECW-bodied VRTs with curved windscreens carried traditional NBC

Right:
A further sign of change was the coming of NBC standard liveries from 1972. Wearing Ribble's traditional deep red and cream is Ribble 2000 (OCK 100K), a 1972 70-seat VRT (left), while alongside is sister vehicle No 2001 after repainting into NBC poppy red and white. Wet conditions prevail as they maintain Carlisle local services. *R. H. G. Simpson*

Centre right:
Some NBC operators clung desperately to their established colours as long as possible. East Yorkshire's buses were traditonally dark blue and primrose, while newly-delivered VRs in 1973 appeared in dark blue but with two white bands (one above the top deck windows), grey wheels and NBC-style fleetnames. DKH 930L (No 930) was so painted and also displays ECW's new curved windscreen and lower front panel. By the end of 1973, NBC red had replaced blue as East Yorkshire's standard colour! *R. H. G. Simpson*

Bottom right:
Another example of ECW's bodywork incorporating a curved windscreen is carried by Greater Manchester 1424 (AJA 424L), finished in orange and white livery and with that operator's own specification of destination display. It was one of 25 6LXB-engined VRT/SLs ordered orginally by the North Western Road Car Co, but delivered in 1973 to SELNEC PTE which had by that time taken over North Western's Cheshire services. The following year SELNEC was itself succeeded by Greater Manchester Transport, following local government reorganisation. *M. S. Curtis*

companies' colours. Earlier VRTs adopted the new liveries when they became due for repainting.

Most ECW bodywork prior to this included cream window rubbers which had been introduced in 1961 as an alternative to black to complement the cream of Tilling and most Scottish group liveries. With the introduction of the NBC's new colours, cream was replaced by grey on ECW bodies, although this was relatively short-lived and by the summer of 1975 black rubber was to be found on all VR bodywork produced at Lowestoft.

Returning to the 1972 Commercial Show, the two remaining VRTs on display were neither ECW-bodied nor for NBC companies, reflecting a growing interest in the model among operators in other sectors. On the Northern Counties stand was a 76-seat body on an 18ft 6in wheelbase VRT/LL chassis, which was among 31 long-wheelbase VRTs built for Reading Corporation. The show example was registered DRD 18L and, with a well designed two-door body with straight staircase, this and the other Reading VRs became known locally as 'Jumbos' due to their size and total capacity (with standees) for over 90 passengers.

The final VRT at the show was another VRT/SL6G model which appeared on the Metro-Cammell Weymann stand in the colours of West Midlands PTE. This was No 4343 (EOF 343L), the first of an initial order for 100 VRTs with 76-seat, single-door bodywork. As with Merseyside, this PTE favoured a design incor-

Right:
An unusual customer for the Bristol VRT during this period was the Department of Environment (whose responsibilities included transport), which received chassis No VRT/SL-2-481 supporting a standard 70-seat ECW body. However, it was not intended for passenger carrying but instead used for driving examiner training purposes. Registered MGP 226L, it is seen here in Bedford during January 1980. This bus was among a large and varied fleet of vehicles by then under the control of the Department of Transport, based with the Driving Examiner Training Establishment at nearby Cardington. *Kevin Lane*

Below right:
Bristol particularly welcomed a request from Hutchings & Cornelius of South Petherton, Somerset, for one VRT/SL6G, as it represented the first VRT order from an independent operator. New in 1973 with ECW bodywork, it is seen here registered RYA 700L, reversing away from the platform at Yeovil bus station when four years old. *M. S. Curtis*

Above:
Another important buyer of the VRT, not least because of the sheer numbers involved, was West Midlands PTE which took 200 Series 2 VRT/SLs into stock. They were fitted with 76-seat bodywork by Metro-Cammell Weymann which, like VRs with other PTEs, featured an engine bustle. Nos 4373 (left) and 4420 appear here on 1 November 1974 at Cannock bus station, where there is clearly no shortage of passengers.
M. S. Curtis

porating a separate engine bustle rather than including the engine within the main body shape. This order was particularly significant for Bristol, as West Midlands PTE normally took locally-built Fleetline rear-engined buses from the Daimler factory located at Coventry.

Reliability of the VRT had greatly improved since its introduction, but work on further improving design details continued. The chassis exhibited on the BCV stand at the 1972 Commercial Show displayed a spring parking brake control which had been repositioned to the right of the driver at window-sill level, while electrical wiring was grouped neatly within protective plastic coverings (with no exposed electrical units) to extend the life of the installations. The electrical features compared very favourably with those of other manufacturers' vehicles and were largely the result of close co-operation with West Midlands PTE engineers, although henceforth applied as standard on all chassis.

By the beginning of 1973, still more buyers were joining the ranks of VRT operators. Sheffield Corporation had received 18 VRT/SLs with 73-seat East Lancs bodywork. Again these featured an engine bustle and were to become part of the South Yorkshire PTE from April 1974, and by the end of that year the first of 50 similar VRT/SLs had been added to the Merseyside PTE fleet, joining the VRT/LHs already in service.

Another PTE, SELNEC, received 25 ECW-bodied VRT/SLs that had originally been ordered by the North Western Road Car Co, whose Greater Manchester Services had been absorbed by SELNEC by the time these buses were due for delivery in 1973.

1973 also saw the first Bristol VRT delivered to an independent operator when a standard VRT/SL6G with 70-seat single-door ECW body was supplied to Hutchings & Cornelius of South Petherton, Somerset (registered RYA 700L), while another, more unusual, order for a single ECW-bodied VRT came from the Department of the Environment, which required one vehicle for driver training purposes. Meanwhile a further municipal order, from an operator well-known as a Bristol customer before sales restrictions were imposed, was received from Cardiff, which sought 20 ECW-bodied VRT/SLs for delivery in 1973/74.

Above:
Eastern Coach Works' ultra-low (13ft 5in tall) bodywork could be easily identified by the lack of waistband over the windscreen. Yorkshire Traction specified this type of bodywork for its first batch of VRTs which included No 804, operating in this view on a service to Pontefract. It is finished in NBC red and white with grey window rubbers.
R. H. G. Simpson

In NBC terms, Hants & Dorset – an ex-Tilling company and important Bristol/ECW customer – took its first VRTs in 1972, while established ex-Tilling VRT operators to place repeat orders for Series 2 models from this period comprised Eastern Counties, Eastern National, Lincolnshire, Midland General (which was henceforth linked to Trent), Southern Vectis, United Automobile, United Counties, West Yorkshire and Western National (which had taken over Devon General). Two other new names from within NBC also appeared in the order books, namely West Riding, which had become part of the THC as recently as 1967, and Alder Valley (which represented a merger between the former Thames Valley (Tilling) and Aldershot & District (BET) companies). Some NBC Bristol VRTs with semi-coach seating could be seen on the streets from this period, with City of Oxford receiving the first such vehicles which entered service from February 1973, wearing a livery incorporating white upper panels and roof – which was a little brighter than the standard NBC layout.

NBC's 1974 vehicle orders (announced the previous summer) listed a requirement for 344 VRTs. This represented a considerable increase over the previous year's requirements, but such was the demand for new double-deckers that these were supplemented by further Atlanteans for certain NBC subsidiaries.

A little over a year later, when NBC published its next round of orders in November 1974, only 100 VRTs were called for. The Treasury had imposed severe public spending cuts and there had also developed a backlog of chassis still to be supplied from previous orders due to component and unit supply problems, which had been exacerbated by the nation's industrial three-day working week. Two more ex-Tilling companies with large Bristol/ECW fleets appeared on the list of VRT customers from the mid-1970s, namely Crosville Motor Services and Cumberland Motor Services, although the former had already operated a number of PMT Bristol VRs on hire. In addition, Maidstone & District took a batch of 14ft 6in high VRT/SLs (in contrast to the earlier ultra-low variants) in 1975, when VRT Series 2 production was drawing to a close.

The design of Bristol's VRT Series 2 was now further improved in terms of reliability. Some operators strove to achieve even better results since rear-engined buses from all manufacturers were generally less dependable and more costly than traditional, front-engined models. For example, Bristol Omnibus experimented by converting some VRTs from semi- to fully-automatic transmission and even conducted tests with Daimler Fleetline rear axles fitted into VRTs to compare their service performance.

In Scotland, however, dissatisfaction with early VRs had never been forgotten. This resulted in the absence of any further SBG orders for VRs (although ECW fared rather better and was favoured with later orders for its VRT-style bodywork – but on Daimler Fleetline chassis!). However, the ultimate disgrace for the VR north of the border followed when the Scottish Bus Group decided preference should be given to running the most reliable double-deck vehicles it could, even with the penalty of having to retain conductors. Conveniently, NBC was taking a different approach and seeking to increase one-man operation. Accordingly, late in 1971, Alexander (Midland) negotiated an exchange, on a one-for-one basis, of all 15 of its VRTs for a similar number of older Bristol/ECW FLF Lodekkas from Eastern National!

By the end of 1972 it was clear the SBG was planning to dispose of all of its VRTs and in January 1973 it was revealed that all except three of SBG's remaining VRTs would be exchanged for more FLFs from throughout the NBC empire. Of the three VRTs not included in this arrangement, two passed to the Essex independent operator, Osborne's of Tollesbury, while the third found its way to a Midlands transport contractor, Richardsons of Oldbury. Nevertheless, no fewer than 106 VRTs

Right:
Further variety provided by NBC's otherwise drab livery policy could be found with City of Oxford (whose vehicles had adopted 'Oxford-South Midland' as a fleetname) with the introduction of a half white/half poppy red scheme in 1973 for a batch of VRTs with 68 semi-coach seats. No 102 exemplifies this layout in Oxford's High Street, whilst heading for Abingdon. *M. S. Curtis*

Below right:
Fifteen VRT/SL6Gs supplied to Maidstone & District during 1975, were the first VRTs to receive ECW 14ft 6in tall 'highbridge' bodywork. These were completed as VRT Series 2 production was drawing to a close, and were readily distinguished by the continuation of their waistband at almost full depth over the windscreen, together with tall lower-deck windows and side panels, as featured by No 5734 (KKE 734N). *M&D and East Kent Bus Club*

were swapped for National Bus Company Lodekkas – with the VRT seemingly doomed to failure in Scotland.

In spite of these problems, the VRT's credibility was improving (and some of the ex-Scottish examples gave many years' service to their new owners). A total of 1,135 Series 2 VRTs had been built, but Leyland, conscious that all of the rear-engined doubled-deck designs produced by its group companies continued to attract criticism, was looking ahead to the development of an advanced double-decker, although this remained some years away from the production stage. Further design improvements for the VRT were therefore allowed to proceed and Bristol was soon to have a model which was not only a great advance from the original VRT, but would also far exceed its predecessors in terms of production levels and sales.

Above right:
The exchange of Scottish Bus Group VRTs for National Bus Company FLFs brought ex-Scottish VRTs to seven NBC subsidiary companies, with a number of the VRs involved giving many years further service with their new owners. Looking immaculate at Norwich bus station just after a repaint in 1978 is Eastern Counties VR328, originally Western SMT 2240. It retains its triangular Scottish destination layout. *M. S. Curtis*

Right:
The Isle of Wight's principal operator, Southern Vectis, also benefited from the FLF/VRT exchange and received three former SBG VRs. Among them was OSF 305G, a VRT/SL6G which was formerly Scottish Omnibuses AA305, but is seen here at Shanklin during August 1973 as Southern Vectis 620. In this case its route number and destination boxes have been rebuilt to side-by-side configuration. *M. S. Curtis*

6
VRT Threes

In the summer of 1974 the trade press was allowed to view a new prototype Bristol/ECW VRT (the chassis of which had been assembled late the previous year). This was to be the first of a new series of double-deckers known as the VRT3, and the bus inspected was shortly to become Western National 1078 (ODV 78M).

This vehicle carried Eastern Coach Works 75-seat bodywork which, although broadly following the pattern of the later Series 2 VRs, clearly displayed features which reflected many of the new design improvements introduced with the VRT3 model. Furthermore, ODV 78M was not powered by the familiar Gardner engine, but instead was fitted with an 8.2-litre Leyland fixed-head, turbo-charged 510 engine, similar to those being installed in Leyland National saloons, although of course fitted vertically in the Bristol VRT.

Great attention had been given to the noise levels produced by this vehicle, largely in anticipation of future legislation, both in the UK and the European Common Market. The entire engine compartment had been completely encapsulated, which not only reduced external noise levels but also enabled the temperature of the engine compartment to be controlled. Ventilation to the engine area remained, of course, but rather than retaining cooling grilles within the engine's side covers, an air intake grille was positioned on the offside of the body below the rearmost upper deck window, and a fan was employed to draw air in through trunking to the engine area. A large air outlet grille was also positioned above the waistband, but this was located on the nearside rear corner, partially facing the rear in order to take full advantage of the natural vacuum which is created behind a moving bus. Internally the air ducts caused a slight size reduction of the parcel shelf behind the lower deck rear bench seat, but this was of little consequence.

Undershield plates enclosed the bottom of the engine compartment while the side and rear engine covers were of a revised pattern. They comprised four glass fibre sections that were mounted independently of the engine frame in order to reduce vibration and maintain a tight fitting. Hinged side panels were similar to those of Series 2 models but the rear centre section, while still hinged at the top, was now a much shorter lift-up flap allowing access to the engine for routine maintenance in confined areas, including between parked vehicles. When necessary, the lower rear section could also be removed completely. At the bottom of the lower panel, the 'Bristol VR' badge was retained in its traditional VRT position while an additional moulding strip had been incorporated into the upper and side engine covers to break-up an otherwise plain area of panelling.

Further attention to noise deadening was also given to the drive shaft, which was housed inside a gaiter where it left the mitre box, although the overall noise reduction was

Above:
ODV 78M, the prototype Bristol VRT3, became Western National 1078. Powered by a turbo-charged Leyland 510 engine, with engine compartment grilles positioned above the waistband, this bus (unlike all subsequent ECW-bodied VRs) retained a Series 2 grille and curved dash panel. It awaits its next trip to Forder in this photograph, taken at Plymouth's Bretonside bus station. *D. Habgood*

Below right:
These are three of the pre-production VRT3s destined for Hants & Dorset, at Bristol's Chatsworth Road works during July 1975. With VRT/SL3/510 chassis designations, these buses clearly display the revised engine cover styling — which formed part of the engine encapsulation — and incorporated a shorter lift-up inspection flap. Also visible are the ventilation grilles above the waistband, linked to the engine compartment by ducting on either side of the rear lower deck window. Allocated fleet Nos (from left to right) 3320, 3319 and 3318, these buses carry registrations JPR 239N, JPR 238N and JJT 433N respectively, but were re-registered KPR 36P, KPR 35P and KRU 439P before entering service. *M. S. Curtis*

never to eliminate the characteristic Bristol transmission whine.

The VRT3 radiator coolant filler cap was placed just above the engine area on the nearside rear, while the radiator remained at the front of the vehicle, but was repositioned a little further forward and angled to improve the flow of air passing over it. The water overflow involved internal piping which rose to the roof on the offside front of the bus.

Transmission in the case of ODV 78M was fully automatic, with Leyland's new G2 control system fitted to the Bristol/Self Changing Gears five-speed unit (although a semi-automatic option would remain). The accelerator followed another pattern previously seen on Leyland group buses as it was of the air-operated type similar to that of the Leyland National.

A further improved rear axle, with redesigned hubs and integral differential, was also incorporated into the VRT3, but one area of the new model not updated was the suspension, with semi-elliptic multiple leaf springs retained front and rear.

Following the appearance of ODV 78M and testing of this vehicle, no fewer than 13 pre-production VRT/SL3s were produced – Bristol perhaps having learned the hard way the importance of thoroughly testing and evaluating a design before full-scale production commenced. The first of the pre-production vehicles was fitted with a Gardner 6LXB power unit while the other 12 continued with the Leyland 500 series engine. The Gardner-powered example received dual-door ECW bodywork and was painted in NBC red livery for Northern General as No 165N (RCN 165N). It appeared in this form on Eastern Coach Works' stand at the 1974 Earls Court Commercial Motor Show held in September, but subsequently entered service re-registered HUP 441N and allocated new fleet No 3239.

This bus largely followed the pattern of the prototype VRT3 (except of course it carried a two-door body with centre staircase), but it displayed one new feature which was not seen on the Western National VRT3, namely a completely revised front grille and dash panel which would henceforth become standard on ECW-bodied VRT3s. The general shape remained similar to that used previously but the grille was no longer slightly recessed and was a little taller than before. The 'Bristol VR' badge was mounted in the centre of the grille for the first time and an oval 'ECW' badge was placed above, although the ECW badge was not included on subsequent VRT3 vehicles.

Also at the 1974 Show, under the Bristol banner, was a VRT3 displayed in chassis form, with turbo-charged Leyland 510 engine developing 155bhp at 2,200rpm. This was to become Southdown 578 (GNJ 578N), one of six pre-production VRT3s for this operator, while the remaining pre-production chassis were allocated to Hants & Dorset.

The chassis type designations and numbering system was slightly revised with the introduction of Series Three VRTs, resulting in the longest type codes ever-carried by Bristol

Right:
Displaying ECW's new grille (with centrally-mounted Bristol VR badge) and dash for the VRT3 is West Riding 756 (NWR 506P), swinging around Wakefield's Bullring. Painted in NBC red livery, it has a standard lowheight body with seating for 74 passengers.
M. S. Curtis

Right:
The 'Bristol VR' grille badge had disappeared from new VRs for NBC subsidiaries by the time London Country received its one and only batch of 15 VRT/SL3/501s in 1977, powered by Leyland 501 engines and carrying highbridge bodywork. The last of the order, BT15 (PPH 475R) is seen in Romford, looking rather incongruous in a fleet which was steeped in London Transport tradition. *M. S. Curtis*

Below right:
A name seen for only a few months on Bristol VRTs was 'Western Welsh', whose HR 1677 stands at Cardiff bus station in October 1977, three months after delivery. This was among the first VRTs received by the Western Welsh and Red & White companies which, although already under common management, were merged to become National Welsh the following year.
M. S. Curtis

vehicles. The main chassis designations (such as VRT/SL) remained as before but were then followed by a '3'; and, instead of the cylinder number and engine manufacturer's initial, a full engine designation was included. A fresh number series commencing at 101 was used for each class of chassis frame. The prototype vehicle was accordingly Type VRT/SL3/510, chassis No 101; while the Northern General pre-production bus became VRT/SL3/6LXB-102.

Full production of Series Three VRs began in 1975 with VRT/SL3/501-115, which became Maidstone & District 5104 (KKO 104P). In contrast to the prototype and pre-production models, the turbo-charged 501 engine (rather than the 510) was employed in production VRT3s with Leyland power units, which was a slightly less powerful version of the 500-series engine. In any event, Gardner-engined VRs found greater favour with operators and many VRTs originally fitted with Leyland engines were later converted to Gardner power.

At approximately the time the VRT3 entered production in 1975, BCV was restyled 'Bristol Commercial Vehicles – Bus Manufacturers Ltd' to reflect the joint British Leyland/National Bus Co ownership of the Brislington bus chassis builders through Bus Manufacturers (Holdings) Ltd. Eastern Coach Works at Lowestoft was similarly retitled, although production at both locations continued much as before. Indeed, so thorough were the design improvements introduced with the new VR that production was to increase substan-

Above:
The introduction of several new double-deck models from other manufacturers prompted NBC to embark on a series of comparative trials between these and Bristol VRTs. Posed here are three of the vehicles involved in such trials at Hastings with Maidstone & District. They are (from left to right) Bristol VRT/SL3/501 No 5104 (KKO 104P) with highbridge ECW bodywork (which was the first production VRT3), No 5382, an Alexander-bodied Volvo-Ailsa, and No 5254, a Scania-based MCW Metropolitan. At the conclusion of the comparative tests it was clear the VRT was a difficult bus to beat! *Ian Allan Library*

tially, far outstripping production levels of earlier VR models. Significantly, the VRT did particularly well against its competitors from this point and it is appropriate to reflect briefly on the other rear-engined double-deck chassis available.

Leyland of course continued to produce the Atlantean which had been updated into its AN68 form from 1972, while the following year Fleetline production was transferred from Daimler in Coventry to Lancashire, where in due course it became the Leyland Fleetline.

For the future, Leyland was working on its integral, highbridge double-deck B15 model, the design of which had been revealed in 1973, with the first prototype completed by the end of 1975. The B15 was intended eventually to replace Atlantean and Fleetline models, with the VRT continuing for the time being as a lowheight double decker.

However, dissatisfaction among operators caused by supply difficulties, and British Leyland's virtual monopoly over the production of double-deckers, had already prompted Metro-Cammell Weymann to collaborate with Scania of Sweden to produce the Metropolitan double-decker. A different approach had been taken by Volvo-Ailsa (again with strong Swedish connections) in the production of a front-engined double-decker suitable for one-man operation, which it hoped would restore a greater degree of confidence in double-deckers in response to the criticism attracted by the unreliability of rear-engined double-deckers in general.

In addition, Dennis and Foden had both declared an intention to enter the market with rear-engined double-deck models, although by this time doubts were being cast about whether demand for new buses could support so many models.

Despite this, VRT3 production was always to be at healthy levels with the established NBC users of the Bristol VR placing substantial orders (including many for Leyland 501-powered examples). National Bus Co orders for the Bristol VRT announced in 1975 totalled 267, then leapt significantly to 529 in 1976, and 531 in 1977 – allowing Bristol's output to remain high despite the run-down of Bristol RE production in favour of the Leyland National. Several additional names from within National Bus were added to the list of VRT customers including East Kent, Yorkshire Woollen District

South Wales Transport and London Country. London Country was established as an NBC subsidiary which inherited the former country services division of London Transport in 1970 with a high proportion of AEC vehicles to London Transport design, and thereafter had added both Leyland Atlantean and Daimler Fleetline double-deckers to its fleet. However, in 1977 one batch of 15 VRT/SLs with Leyland 501 engines and highbridge ECW 74-seat coachwork entered service. Although unusual vehicles for London Country, they reflected more closely NBC's approach to bus design standards. They remained unique in the London Country fleet and lasted only three to four years before transfer to the Bristol Omnibus Co. Finally, another new name carried by NBC group VRTs was National Welsh, following the 1978 merger of Red & White Services with Western Welsh (both of which had only just before received their first Bristol VRs).

Aside from NBC, other important orders were received for VRT3s. In 1976 it was announced that 25 VRT/LLs were required by Tayside Regional Council for delivery the following year. These were specified with Alexander 83-seat dual-door bodywork but, more importantly, would once again take the Bristol VR to a customer in Scotland. Reading Transport also took 19 further VRT/LLs to add to its fleet of Northern Counties-bodied 'Jumbo' buses in 1976/77, but, unlike Reading's earlier lowheight VRs, these were built to an interim height of 14ft 2in. owing to a local height restriction having been relaxed.

VRT/SL chassis were also sought after by municipalities. Five Gardner 6LX-engined examples with ECW bodywork entered service with City of Lincoln in 1975, followed by a further five similar vehicles but with 6LXB power units in 1976. Meanwhile, Burnley & Pendle took East Lancs 75-seat coachwork on a batch of 14 VRT/SL3/6LXBs delivered in 1976, while no fewer than 36 VRT/SLs were requested by Northampton, to be fitted with Alexander dual-door bodies.

Another new customer was Cleveland Transit, which in 1977 received 15 VRT/SLs with Gardner engines and Northern Counties coachwork, while Great Yarmouth supported ECW, its local bodybuilder, when ordering eight VRTs for delivery the same year. Cardiff also returned to Bristol for more VRTs, but unlike previous VRs for the Welsh capital, these carried highbridge bodywork by Willowbrook, incorporating a frontal design which attempted to emulate that of ECW. Due to an overwhelming level of orders at ECW, Willowbrook also built similar VRT bodies for NBC's East Kent and Northern General subsidiaries during the late 1970s.

However, perhaps the most unexpected VRT customer during this period was the Atomic Energy Research Establishment at Harwell, which became a Bristol user when three ECW-bodied VRTs were purchased for staff transport in 1977, to be followed by a small but regular intake of Bristol/ECW double-deckers in successive years.

The arrival on the scene of several new double-deck models prompted the National Bus Co to embark on a series of trials to compare these with standard Bristol VRTs. It was therefore arranged for comparisons to be

Right:
Northern Counties, having already bodied examples of the VRT Series 2 chassis, supplied further coachwork to its sturdy but angular design on VRT3s during the mid-1970s. Among its customers was Cleveland Transit, which called for 15 Gardner 6LXB-engined VRT/SLs, and whose H102 pauses in Albert Road, Middlesbrough during July 1981. *M. S. Curtis*

Right:
Reading became an important Bristol customer. Having already received 31 Series 2 VRT/LLs, it ordered a further 19 VRT/LL3/6LXBs. Again these supported Northern Counties bodywork but were constructed to a slightly taller overall height of 14ft 2in and, as exemplified by No 44 seen in Reading's Broad Street, were finished in maroon and white livery. From 1 January 1973 most British motor vehicles were compelled to carry reflective registration plates rather than the former design with white or silver characters on black. However, Reading was one of several bus operators to take advantage of an exemption for buses used on local services. *M. S. Curtis*

Centre right:
An extraordinary scene was that of Bristol VRT chassis on a railway truck. Normally, chassis were driven for test or delivery purposes but lengthy delays at W. Alexander & Co (Coachbuilders) in bodying a number of VRTs for Northampton resulted in their return to Bristol by rail, where they were checked by BCV before returning to Scotland for bodying. Two such chassis await unloading at Lawrence Hill goods yard, Bristol in November 1977. By a coincidence, the Bristol Omnibus Central Repair Works appears in the background — hence the 'Bristol' scroll on the nearest building. *M. S. Curtis*

Bottom right:
Between June 1977 and October 1978 Northampton introduced 36 Alexander-bodied VRT/SLs, whose two-door bodies seated 72. No 41 was among the earliest to be delivered, seen working on route 8 at St Giles' Square, Northampton. *M. S. Curtis*

Right:
Throughout the period of VRT3 production the majority of chassis were standard VRT/SL models for National Bus Company operators, usually with ECW bodywork. This Trent example represents hundreds of similar vehicles found throughout England and Wales wearing standard NBC livery. Even its one-piece destination display had itself become an NBC standard from 1976. No 822 (URB 822S) appears in this view at Uttoxeter. *M. S. Curtis*

made with tests conducted under strictly controlled conditions, the first of which commenced in February 1976 at Maidstone & District's Hastings Silverdale depot. There, five Scania-powered Metropolitans and five front-engined Volvo-Ailsas were to be evaluated alongside four highbridge-bodied Bristol/ECW VRT3s, two of which were powered by Gardner 6LX (150 bhp) units while the other pair were fitted with Leyland 501 (170 bhp) engines. After one year's comparative trials, the Gardner-engined VRTs were found to be by far the most economical of the 14 buses. These vehicles were then moved to Chatham for further tests which confirmed the Gardner VRTs as the most fuel efficient, with the Leyland-engined versions taking second place.

A full report followed, which indicated that the Gardner-engined VRTs not only had the lowest operating costs but were also the most reliable. It was recognised that this Bristol model would be difficult to better when the time came to find a successor. When these details were released towards the end of 1978, another phase of NBC trials had commenced with Potteries Motor Traction where ECW-bodied VRTs were compared with two more newcomers, the Dennis Dominator and Northern Counties-Foden double-deck designs. It soon became clear that despite the diverse nature of operating conditions throughout the NBC subsidiaries, the standard NBC Bristol VRT bus was the model with which others had to compete.

Meanwhile, in Scotland, Tayside had been conducting similar tests in Dundee during 1977 with a Volvo-Ailsa, a Gardner-engined Daimler Fleetline and a Bristol VRT/LL, also with a Gardner power unit. All three types carried Alexander bodywork, but in these trials the results suggested greater vehicle availability existed with the front-engined model.

By 1976, a subtle change of emphasis had been introduced by the badges carried on new Bristol-built vehicles for service with the National Bus Company, to move away from the Bristol name. From this time the NBC double-N symbol, which originally and like the company fleetname had been in white on the main paintwork of buses, was replaced by a red and blue version (similar to that already carried on coaches). It was positioned within a white box, ahead of the fleetnames and often elsewhere on vehicles – such as on the front grille. All this was designed to promote the NBC identity even more strongly than before. Presumably to avoid conflict between this symbol and manufacturers' badges, it was

Right:
Whilst, in general, NBC buses were required to carry standard red or green colours, there were some notable exceptions. In the Northeast, both Northern General and United Automobile vehicles operating within the Tyne & Wear PTE area were required to adopt yellow liveries to match the PTE's own buses. Accordingly, United 707 emerges from Eldon Square bus station, Newcastle, in July 1981, wearing a refreshingly attractive yellow and white livery but with NBC-style fleetnames. *M. S. Curtis*

decided that Bristol VRTs (and LHs) built for NBC with ECW bodywork would no longer be permitted to carry 'Bristol' badges on their radiator grilles! Bristol motifs on VRT wheel hubs for NBC customers were also no longer applied with the previous degree of thoroughness, but the 'Bristol VR' badge on rear engine covers remained, since these were applied at Bristol as part of the chassis, rather than at ECW! Ironically, ECW-bodied VRs for other operators (together with VRs bodied by other coachbuilders) continued to display a full complement of manufacturers' badges, and one wonders what NBC sought to achieve by pursuing its obsession with corporate identity to this extent.

One of the first buses to carry the new NBC symbols appeared at the 1976 Commercial Motor Show (which was the last such exhibition to be held at Earls Court). There, Lincolnshire VRT 1925 (RFE 66R) could be seen on ECW's stand next to a Bristol LHS saloon for Trent. Bristol's own display at the Show, which was completely integrated with that of British Leyland, consisted only of an LHS chassis.

Such was the popularity of the VRT3 that by the end of 1979 over 2,000 VRT3 chassis had been completed, exceeding the combined totals for all previous VR types – and orders continued to flow in, with the VRT3 outselling every other rear-engined double-deck model in 1980, with more than 600 produced

Right:
Willowbrook highbridge bodywork was built on VRT/SLs for Cardiff Corporation, East Kent and Northern General. Whilst frontal styling was clearly influenced by ECW, in other respects an upright but well-proportioned vehicle resulted. In immaculate condition just after entry into service, Cardiff 314 (SWO 314S), wearing orange and white paintwork, stops in Wood Street during early January 1978. *M. S. Curtis*

that year. Of course, since the VR remained its standard double-decker, the National Bus Company accounted for much of the production requirements with 465 ordered in 1978 (323 with Gardner engines, the remainder powered by Leyland) and a further 498 the following year, but other operators too specified Bristol VRTs.

In 1978, A. Mayne & Son of Manchester had become the first independent operator of VRT3s when three VRT/SL3/6LXBs with ECW coach-seated bodies were received. In the municipal sector, Lincoln returned for four more VRT/SLs with East Lancs bodies in 1979, to add to the 10 ECW-bodied examples it already had in service. Conversely, during the previous year, Burnley & Pendle added 10 ECW-bodied VRT3s to its fleet of 14 East Lancs-bodied Bristol VRs. Great Yarmouth bought four further ECW VRT/SLs in 1979, while Cardiff, although switching to Alexander for its bodywork, continued to receive substantial numbers of VRT/SLs.

Rather than holding separate motor shows for cars and commercial vehicles as had been the case at Earls Court, the events were combined from 1978 and the venue moved to the newly-opened National Exhibition Centre, Birmingham. Here, a Bristol VRT was to appear at such a show for the last time when a standard NBC VRT/SL example in green United Counties livery (No 904; CBD 904T) was displayed among the Leyland exhibits.

This bus displayed a number of new detail differences which represented the final development stage for both the chassis and the standard design of ECW body. New versions of the hopper and sliding ventilators were incorporated into the windows, and whilst similar to those fitted previously, the hopper vents in particular were noticeably longer than before.

Below left:
Another municipality to purchase significant numbers of Bristol VRs was Lincoln. Originally introduced wearing light green and cream, a revised livery of off-white and green stripes had been adopted prior to this photograph being taken in the summer of 1991. ECW-bodied VRT/SL No 28 stands flanked by two East Lancs-bodied VRs: VRT/LL 41 (left) and VRT/SL 34 (right). Lincoln's ECW-bodied VRTs carried both 'Bristol VR' and 'ECW' badges, as seen here. *M. S. Curtis*

Below right:
The ubiquitous VRT/SL was to be found at locations all over the country, among the most easterly being those wearing the blue and cream colours of Great Yarmouth Borough Transport. No 32 (RVF 32R) accelerates out of Regent Street one October evening in 1986, bound for the District Hospital. Eastern Coach Works bodywork was a natural choice for this customer, in view of its proximity to Lowestoft. *M. S. Curtis*

As was previously the case, these were produced by Widney Windows, rather than ECW itself.

Inside, a new interior decor was applied which included upholstery in orange and black moquette, which could be specified in preference to the plain and uninviting plastic seating covering, and superseded the red and green moquette styles previously used as standard for NBC by Eastern Coach Works.

In the cab, a new design of steering wheel dispensed with the 'Bristol' badge in the centre, although a traditional 'Bristol' scroll continued to be carried in the vehicle – tucked away on the foot brake pedal, defiantly opposing NBC and Leyland's policy of reducing the prominence of the Bristol name!

Two final detail changes, which did not apply to the Show bus but followed on ECW bodies from 1980, were the replacement of the gently curved indicator/stop/tail/side light clusters with rather more severe, square designs – which didn't really match ECW's body lines – and the use of new cab heaters which needed a small exterior breather grille near the cab on the offside.

Bristol VR production continued apace even though work was by now progressing at Bristol on a replacement double-deck design. In addition to NBC, Cardiff, Great Yarmouth and Northampton were among loyal customers placing repeat orders, with Cardiff amassing no fewer than 117 Bristol VRTs to become the municipal operator with by far the largest fleet of VRTs. Rhymney Valley was another local authority operator to be added to the list of VRT customers when three East Lancs-bodied examples were purchased in 1981, joining the VRTs inherited by that organisation from Gelligaer.

Stevensons, the famous independent based at Spath, Uttoxeter, also became a VRT operator from late 1980, while perhaps the most unlikely VRT order was placed through Leyland Netherlands by the Sijthoff Pers newspaper group of Rijswijk, which required a double-decker for publicity purposes. Although carrying an ECW ultra-low body, low profile wheels and tyres were also fitted in order to conform with local requirements to achieve the lowest possible overall height. Special opening windows were also included, and internally, it was fitted with a kitchen and VIP reception area. This bus could be seen at special events promoting different newspaper titles, as appropriate for the event and location.

Despite the success of the VRT3, the Bristol VR's image in Scotland was again to be severely tarnished by the announcement, during the summer of 1980, that in the interests of fleet standardisation, Tayside, Scotland's only remaining VR operator and its only customer for the VRT3, was to dispose of all 25 of its VRT/LLs after only three years of service! This was devastating news and surely confirmed that the VR was destined never to succeed north of the border. As before, the Scottish VRs were snapped up readily by English and Welsh operators including Burnley & Pendle, Lincoln City Transport, National Welsh (Red & White), Osborne's of Tollesbury and Tally Ho! in Devon.

Elsewhere, however, the VR continued to do well, but in October 1980 Bristol's new dou-

Right:
A. Mayne & Son Ltd, an independent operator based in Manchester, bought three coach-seated VRT/SL3/6LXBs in 1978, including VJA 665S. Two more similar VRTs followed in 1980. Compared with earlier VRT3s, the rear engine cover flap had been modified to accommodate advertising posters by lowering the central moulding strip and moving the emergency engine-stop button further to the offside.
ECW

Right:
The introduction of 25 Bristol VRT/LLs by Tayside Regional Council from February to March 1977 brought Bristol VRs back to Scotland. Twenty of the batch had Gardner 6LXB engines while the remaining five were Leyland 501-powered. All received Alexander's heavy-looking 83-seat dual-door bodywork. OSR 195R (No 195) is depicted in Dundee. *C. L. Caddy*

Centre right:
Perhaps the most elusive Bristol VRTs were those used for staff transport by the Atomic Energy Research Establishment at Harwell. Special permission was sought to photograph these two VRT/SL3/6LXBs preparing for an out-muster in September 1989. Despite being 11 years old, low mileage and high standards of maintenance were evident, with even the 'Bristol' hub badges remaining intact in this picture. Altogether seven VRTs were supplied to Harwell AERE, whose vehicles were painted blue and grey. *M. S. Curtis*

Bottom right:
Burnley & Pendle purchased new VRT/SLs with both East Lancs and ECW coachwork, plus further second-hand examples with Alexander bodywork from Tayside. No 156 is a VRT/SL3/6LXB with an East Lancs 75-seat highbridge body, at Burnley in August 1978. *M. S. Curtis*

Right:
The only Bristol VRT to be exported new was chassis No VRT/SL3/6LXB-2149 which, at the end of 1979, was sold through Leyland Netherlands to the Sijthoff Pers newspaper group. Carrying licence No 74-TB-57, its ECW bodywork lacked usual interior fittings and was equipped with a kitchen and VIP reception area for use in supporting or promoting events in The Hague area. Low profile wheels and tyres reduced the ultra-low body height still further, while a profusion of fully-hinged opening windows also modified its appearance.
Sijthoff Pers

ble-deck chassis, the B45 (Olympian), was officially launched, with full production commencing at BCV's Brislington works early the following year. VRTs and Olympians were produced side-by-side for some months thereafter but only orders for the Olympian double-decker were being accepted and the end was in sight for the Bristol VRT. Even at this late stage, however, two new VRT models surprisingly appeared!

The first was the VRT/SL3/6LXC, with slightly more powerful Gardner engine, which was fitted to some VRTs in the final months of VR production. The second model was the VRT/SL3/680 powered by Leyland's well established 0.680 unit which was unexpectedly fitted to the final batches of VRTs for Bristol Omnibus and Southdown in order to relieve a critical shortage of Gardner engines, so that the chassis could be released.

The last long wheelbase VRT/LL buses were also built early in 1981 as part of an order for Lincoln City for seven such chassis with Gardner 6LXB engines and East Lancs 86-seat coachwork. Then, in August, Bristol ceased building the VRT altogether in favour of the Olympian, although bodywork on the final VR chassis was not completed by Eastern Coach Works at Lowestoft until the end of the year. The last VRT-style bodies produced by ECW were actually built on the last two Fleetline chassis constructed – rather than Bristol VRTs – at the end of 1981 for the South Notts Bus Co.

The final Bristol VRT, with chassis No VRT/SL3/6LXB 3101, became Stevensons 49 (UVT 49X), its second new VRT with ECW 70-seat double-deck coach bodywork, which brought the closing total of VRT3 production to 3,052. The penultimate chassis, No 3100, was in fact the last for an NBC operator, becoming Eastern Counties VR294 (VEX 294X). Since, significantly, this was for ECW's local operator, it was carefully arranged for this bus to be the last VR finished at Lowestoft.

Bristol VRT production reached a grand total of 4,474 when adding Series 1 and 2 chassis; the majority, of course, for National Bus Company fleets. The single most important Bristol VRT customer was the Western National group, which took 244 examples from all three series of chassis, closely followed by Crosville which, although introducing VRTs much later, nevertheless bought 243, only one less than Western National. Southdown (including Brighton Hove & District) was the third largest buyer with 234 VRTs purchased new, while Bristol Omnibus, Eastern Counties, United Automobile and United Counties were also important NBC group customers with over 200 VRTs delivered new to each.

Major customers outside of the National Bus Company organisation included the West Midlands and Merseyside PTEs which received 200 and 110 VRTs respectively, while 10 municipalities accepted new Bristol VRTs into stock.

Right:
This is not quite what it appears at first glance. Although conveying the appearance of a new VRT3, the G-suffix registration carried by United Counties 752, pictured here at Leighton Buzzard in 1981, belies the fact that this is actually a 1969 Series 1 VRT. It was among several early VRTs rebuilt by United Counties to what was described as 'Series 3' standards, although this stopped short of encapsulating the engine compartment. *Kevin Lane*

The Bristol VR had successfully thrust aside the image of a problematical bus that it had begun to attract in its earliest days, to become, through rapid and sound development, a double-decker known to millions of travellers throughout England and Wales. And in addition to those acquired second-hand from Scotland, many operators (especially in the NBC group) took the opportunity to add further to their VRT fleets as inevitable changes in service levels released examples from some areas. As still more become available on occasions, these too continue to attract eager buyers, including many new operators of the type.

The Bristol VRT is still to be seen about the country in vast numbers, many still operating with their original owners, and it is most probable that this model will remain familiar well into the 21st century.

Right:
The last Bristol VR ever built (with chassis No VRT/SL3/6LXB-3101) became Stevensons 49 (UVT 49X) in October 1981. It had an ECW coach-seated body with square indicator/side light clusters as fitted by ECW to the final VRs, together with a split-level entrance similar to those seen experimentally on VRTs eight years earlier. Operating in Stevensons' yellow, black and white colours, No 49 was caught by the camera in Birmingham in April 1982. Six years later this bus passed to Midland Fox, before being sold again to Crosville Wales in 1992. *Rex Kennedy*

7

Open-Top VRs

By the time Bristol's VRT had entered production, a tradition had been established among some operators to provide summer services using open-top double-deckers – usually at coastal resorts. Of course when early double-deck motorbuses had become common, in the 1900s, they had been open on the top deck – as had most trams and double-deck horsebuses that preceded them. Gradually, however, designs evolved to include lower chassis and covered top-deck accommodation.

The authorities in London were slower than many to accept that covered top double-deckers could operate safely, and it was not until 1925 that buses entered service in the capital with fully enclosed seating on their upper decks. In the provinces, attitudes were generally more relaxed but in Cheltenham, for example, covered-top double-deckers were not allowed in the town prior to 1934 – on aesthetic grounds! Nevertheless, by the end of the decade all conventional British double-deckers were constructed with fully enclosed bodywork.

The idea of running special open-top buses began to regain popularity after World War 2, and experiments commenced around the country, in almost every case at seaside locations where advantage could be taken of the postwar boom in holiday traffic.

The Bristol Tramways company decided to embark upon such a scheme and inaugurated a new sea-front service at Weston-super-Mare in 1950, using AEC Regents converted to open-top layout. Ironically, these AECs were non-standard vehicles which Bristol had just acquired with the Cheltenham District fleet, having been among the first Cheltenham buses ever built with covered top-deck bodywork! Although the Weston-super-Mare service was an immediate success, the AEC vehicles were replaced by rather more standard Bristol K-type open-toppers over the next few years.

Elsewhere, open-top coastal services were proving very popular and many operators ran them, including Devon General, using AEC Regents in the Torquay area; Western and Southern National with Bristol K-types for services such as those at Bridport, Falmouth and Newquay; Hants & Dorset employing Leyland and Bristol open-toppers with either full-front or removable-top bodywork; and Southern Vectis with AEC and Bristol vehicles for use on the Isle of Wight. Brighton Hove & District was an early operator of open-top services with AEC and Bristol vehicles, including those with its own design of convertible open-top bodies, while neighbouring Sussex operator Southdown maintained coastal routes with open-top Guy Arabs, as did East Kent. Inland, Thames Valley provided a service from Reading to Maidenhead following the Thames via Henley and Marlow using Bristol K5Gs acquired from Brighton Hove & District.

Moving to East Anglia, more open-toppers (including Bristols) could be found with Westcliff-on-Sea Motor Services (AEC Regents, a Dennis Lance and Bristol G-types) and East-

Right:
This is one of 50 VRT/SLs built with ECW convertible open-top bodywork for NBC subsidiaries. Painted in standard NBC red bus livery, this was the first of six allocated to Hants & Dorset, and as fleet No 3374 was later registered UFX 855S. These vehicles received an extra drainage slot, visible on the waistband in this September 1977 photograph, taken just before delivery. *ECW*

ern Counties (G- and K-types), while Eastern National ran AEC, Bristol and Leyland open-toppers.

Similar stories were repeated around the country with many more companies involved in open-top operations, together with a large number of municipal concerns, particularly in the South of England. In many fleets open-toppers were among the oldest buses, having been retained for summer use only (after conversion). The majority carried a predominantly cream livery, which soon became associated with this kind of holiday operation and increased the prominence of the special services they provided.

Although the idea of having double-deck bodywork with detachable tops had already been seen on Bristols with Brighton Hove & District and Hants & Dorset, 1956 saw the first new Bristols built with convertible bodywork. This dispensed with the notion that open-toppers had to be among the older members of the

Below:
In early 1979, after spending little more than a year with Hants & Dorset, the six UFX-registered VRT3 open-toppers were transferred to Southern Vectis, in exchange for six conventional VRT3s. Before crossing to the Isle of Wight, where they were quickly set to work on the island's busy open-top services, these convertible VRs were repainted NBC green (but with white extending above the waistband). Climbing away from Shanklin Esplanade during August 1980, as Southern Vectis 707, is UFX 857S, heavily laden with passengers. *M. S. Curtis*

Above:
Eleven convertible VRT3s were dispatched to the Western National group where, regardless of whether they carried Western National or Devon General lettering, all carried NBC red livery with much more white than usual. Known as the 'Warship' class because each was allocated the name of a Warship, Devon General's 942 (*Hermes*) and 940 (*Invincible*) are viewed here in Torquay during 1978, their first year in service. *M. S. Curtis*

fleet since, when not required in open-top form, they could continue in normal service with tops replaced.

Eastern Coach Works built eight convertible bodies on LD-type Lodekkas for Crosville in 1956, followed three years later by a further six. All were used on North Wales coastal routes. Bristol Omnibus bought four Bristol ECW FS-type convertible Lodekkas in 1961 for operations at Weston-super-Mare, while in the same year Devon General introduced its 'Sea Dog' class of Leyland Atlanteans, which consisted of nine vehicles (each carrying the name of a famous seafarer) with Metro-Cammell bodies featuring detachable roofs. Convertible Bristol/ECW Lodekkas were also favoured by Brighton Hove & District, with no fewer than 16 entering its fleet from 1959 to 1964, while Southdown opted for 30 convertible Leyland Titan PD3s with Northern Counties bodywork, in the 1960s.

Open-top services generally continued to be popular, but in some areas interest waned in the interim before a resurgence of enthusiasm, while other operators turned their attention in the 1970s to inland open-top tourist services which could offer excellent views for visitors. In many cases, open-top fleets were again falling due for replenishment, with operators looking to convert services generally to one-man operation where possible.

With several established open-top bus operators now within the National Bus Company, and with VRT3 production in 'full swing', the time was ripe to allow NBC companies the opportunity to introduce a new generation of Bristol open-top bus, with the construction by Eastern Coach Works of a batch of convertible VRT3s.

Fifty such vehicles were completed by ECW in 1977-78, on VRT/SL chassis (the majority with Gardner 6LXB engines). They had jig-built removable tops (which were interchangeable between VRTs of this batch) and fixings for tall rails and screens to allow safe operation in open-top form without a conductor. At just under 14ft with roofs in position, these bodies were almost 4in taller than ECW's standard, representing a fourth height variant for Bristol VR bodywork built at Lowestoft. Instead of the cream livery of earlier years, all were received wearing NBC standard colours of poppy red or leaf green (with white) but some operators applied daring variations – by increasing the areas painted white!

Four NBC companies were allocated these vehicles initially, with no fewer than 30 requested by Southdown (which by this time had absorbed Brighton Hove & District). Of these, 10 (somewhat surprisingly) were of dual-door layout with centre stairs.

Eleven were destined for the Western National group to form a new 'Warship' class of named buses for use on both Devon General and Western National services.*Regardless of the fleetname carried, all were finished in red and white livery. Hants & Dorset received six which, with the exception of an appearance at the 1978 Derby, received little use as open-toppers and, after only one season, were transferred across the Solent to the Isle of Wight in exchange for six standard VRT/SLs from Southern Vectis. The remaining three convertible ECW-bodied VRTs – which were the only examples with Leyland 501 engines – went to South Wales Transport.

The single-door, convertible VRs were notable for having a slightly different top-deck seating arrangement. On standard ECW-bodied VRTs, three forward-facing single seats were fitted alongside the stair-well on the upper deck but on the convertibles only two such seats were fitted behind a side-facing double seat.

This conveniently overcame difficulties with passengers' feet hitting the front door-gear cover box and squeezed one additional seat in on the nearside. To allow sufficient leg-room, the front facing bench seat normally suitable for three persons was replaced with a double seat, offering no overall benefit other than a marginally improved top-deck view through the driver's periscope.

Conspicuously absent among the recipients of new convertible VRTs was Bristol Omnibus, which had delayed making a decision on the replacement of its expanded open-top fleet of front-engined Bristols at Weston-super-Mare, added to which was an LD Lodekka used on a City of Bristol open-top tour. When a decision was finally made in 1979 to progress the conversion of services to one-man operation using rear-engined double-deckers, a mixed selection of second-hand, non-standard Atlanteans and Fleetlines was acquired from Hants & Dorset, Maidstone & District and Midland Red, all of which had to be rebuilt as permanent open-toppers in Bristol's own works.

Bristol's requirements for open-top buses was not satisfied, however, and although Southern Vectis needed a substantial number of open-toppers during the summer months, it was agreed in 1983 that two of its convertible VRs (which had originated with Hants & Dorset) should again be transferred, this time to Bristol Omnibus for use in Weston-super-Mare, in return for two standard VRTs bought new by Bristol.

Further west, most of Western National's open-toppers were allocated to its Devon General services, but open-top buses were also provided under Western National's name in Cornwall and in Dorset. There one open-topper was made available for use at Weymouth depot during the peak summer, usually following the annual Epsom Derby which was attended by the Devon General open-toppers. Although previously an Atlantean had been allocated, in 1982 a VRT (No 934, named *Golden Hind*) was diverted to Weymouth for summer use, on return from Epsom.

From 1 January 1983, the Western National group was divided into four new operating companies with the new, smaller Western National Ltd retaining four convertible VRTs in Cornwall, while Devon General continued to hold five more. Southern National, which was resurrected to take over Somerset and Dorset services, not only retained No 934 but also acquired No 942 for Weymouth use. What is more, these two were rapidly repainted into a Tilling cream and NBC green colour scheme (but with NBC style fleetnames) which made a refreshing contrast to the usual NBC shades.

Meanwhile, the two convertible VRTs with Bristol Omnibus had received a remarkably similar livery in Bath, where they had been transferred following the successful establishment of a Bath city tour, and such was the demand for more open-top VRTs with both Bristol and Southern National, that Hants & Dorset Engineering was engaged in rebuilding earlier VRTs to permanent open-top form (which included providing a waterproof top-deck floor!) for both operators.

Conversions of Bristol VRs to permanent open-top layout was to become widespread

Right:
Upon the division of Western National Omnibus Co in 1983, two of the 'Warship' class convertibles passed to Southern National Ltd for use at Weymouth. They were daringly repainted leaf green with Tilling cream, and renamed after personalities with Dorset connections. Pictured at Bowleaze Cove in open-top form is No 934 (VDV 134S), christened *Thomas Hardy*, while behind with roof in position is No 942 (VDV 142S) again, now renamed *Lawrence of Arabia*. *M. S. Curtis*

Centre right:
South Wales Transport received three of the original convertible VRT3s which were the only Leyland 501-engined versions. Finished in NBC red when new, No 930 (RTH 930S) is seen at Tenby in 1988 when 11 years old, wearing SWT's later light green and lime livery. Once again a name is carried – in this case *Dylan Thomas*. *M. .S. Curtis*

Bottom right:
ECW's customer for the largest number of convertible VRT3s was Southdown, which received 30 including some built to dual-door layout. During the mid-1980s Southdown was divided, leading to the revival of a Brighton & Hove company, and several of the convertible VRTs passed into this fleet to receive a modernised red and cream Brighton & Hove livery. Among them was UWV 615S (No 615), seen here at Brighton Old Steine in 1990. To its credit, Southdown was among few NBC companies to persevere with rear route number displays, arranged as shown in this view. Full use of the advertising spaces on this bus is also demonstrated. *M. S. Curtis*

Above:
A pair of Series 1 VRT/LLs, among those originally supplied to Eastern Scottish, became the only long-wheelbase VRT open-top buses when converted by Alder Valley. Their top-deck seating capacity was just 43, rather less than when built, which failed to take full advantage of the extra length available. They were employed on a route following the course of the Thames between Marlow and Windsor. LFS 288F had become Alder Valley 895 when photographed at Windsor in 1983.
G. B. Wise

around the country. This often involved older vehicles that were written down in value, and occasionally 'rebuilding' buses after they had been victims of lowbridge accidents! However, in addition to the batch of 50 ECW convertible bodies on VRs, two further VRTs were built new with convertible open-top bodywork. These were specified by City of Cardiff, whose 1979 Alexander-bodied VRT/SLs Nos 359 and 360 arrived as convertible open-toppers.

While not limited to coastal services, the value and popularity of providing open-top buses for city sightseeing or special duties and private hires grew considerably in the 1980s with many more VRTs selected to meet the resurgence of interest. A large number of flat-front, ECW-bodied VRTs (from both Series 1 and 2) was converted to open-top, including former Scottish examples used for United's sea-front services at Scarborough, ex-West Yorkshire buses made available by NBC's Amalgamated Passenger Transport (APT) engineering unit, and ex-Ribble examples with Eastern Counties. Trent's 1969 VRT No 757, inherited from Midland General, became 'topless' in 1984, while ex-West Yorkshire flat-front VRs could also be found with Cityrama on London Sightseeing. The only VRT/LL models converted to open-top were a pair of ex-Eastern Scottish examples which ran with Alder Valley South and Berks Bucks Bus Co respectively, having previously been members of the Thames Valley & Aldershot (Alder Valley) fleet. Oxford's VRT No 901 (OFC 901H), the first Series 2 VRT/SL and the first bus built as part of an order for an NBC subsidiary, was also converted to open-top having been renumbered 301. Further VRTs, of the curved-screen Series 2 variety, emerged in open-top form too. Among companies with VRTs of this style were Alder Valley, Cambus, Eastern Counties, Eastern National, Hastings & District, South Midland and United Auto, with many carrying more varied liveries than earlier as NBC livery policy gradually became more relaxed, followed by the privatisation of this organisation.

Inevitably, still more Series 3 VRTs were converted to open-top to add to those already described, with the Bristol VR bus becoming the most widely used open-top model in Britain. Of these, one of the most unusual was East Kent's No 0977 (RVB 977S) with Willowbrook bodywork, which became an open-topper in 1981 following a 'low-bridge' accident. Further north, inland operator East Midland converted a VRT3 to topless layout for use on special occasions, while in York, one of several open-deck VRs seen in that city was a VRT3 (HWJ 924W) which had been rebuilt as a convertible, and borrowed from Yorkshire Traction in 1984.

Some years later, a number of companies had become part of the Stagecoach group and there followed a series of vehicle transfers between fleets. As a result, Southdown VRT convertibles could be found in the Lake District working for Cumberland (but retaining their delightful apple green and cream livery), while two more examples even appeared in Scotland – with Stagecoach at Inverness.

In Wales, two further VRT3s – belonging to National Welsh as HR817 and HR818 (VHB 677S and VHB 678S) – were rebuilt in 1986 to convertible open-top form. They were perhaps the least used open-toppers of all convertible VRs until transferred to Crosville Wales in 1990, where they joined three permanent open-top VRT3s converted from Crosville's own fleet, for use along the North Wales coast.

There are too many other locations where open-top VRTs have been introduced to list them all here separately. However, several are worthy of special mention. In Sussex, where the largest concentration of convertible VRs remained, the division of Southdown (followed by privatisation) saw the resurrection of red and cream Brighton & Hove buses to complement the green and cream of Southdown – although later takeover by Stagecoach saw Southdown's traditional colours replaced by a white-based scheme.

Wilts & Dorset, Hants & Dorset's successor in the resorts of Bournemouth and Swanage, built up an open-top fleet again in the late 1980s after the disposal of the original convertible VRTs. While most of these were rebuilt Olympian double-deckers, one more VRT was included.

Along the coast, further expansion of the open-top fleet followed at Southern National

Below left:
Seen at Epsom for a Derby is East Kent's unique Willowbrook-bodied open-top VRT/SL No 0977 (RVB 977S) which was rebuilt to open-top following a 'lowbridge' accident in 1980. The seaside service it normally provides is advertised on the 'between-decks' panelling. *M. S. Curtis*

Below right:
Following the batch of convertibles built by ECW, only two further VRTs were produced new with convertible open-top bodywork. These were supplied to Cardiff Corporation in 1979, with Alexander bodywork. This April 1987 picture shows VRT/SL No 359 (WTG 359T) entering Cardiff's busy Duke Street, with its roof removed. *M. S. Curtis*

with a gradual change of livery to yellow, blue and orange/red. Meanwhile the Stratford-upon-Avon based tourism specialist, Guide Friday Ltd, expanded throughout Britain to provide a fleet of open-toppers offering guided tours of historic cities and towns, with several acquired VRTs within its varied fleet; while City Line in Bristol inevitably used VRs for its City of Bristol tour, working in conjunction with Guide Friday during 1991/92.

Aside from Sussex, the largest concentration of open-top Bristol VRs (including both convertible and permanently open vehicles) could be found in Bath, where the dominance of such buses resulted in the local authority seeking limits on their numbers! Here, Badgerline had inherited the former Bristol Omnibus operation and after a brief period of its six open-toppers carrying blue, red and yellow Roman City livery, 'The Bath Tour' fleet was repainted primrose, with Brunswick-green and lime green relief from 1989 – from which year Guide Friday also provided guides and support for the tours. By the 1991 season, no fewer than 12 VRTs could be found in Bath owing to a spectacular increase in Badgerline's open-top business, despite the appearance of competition. In addition to the convertibles from Southern Vectis and three permanent open-top VRs rebuilt for Bath use, other Badgerline group companies provided additional vehicles, with two transferred from City Line, two from South Wales Transport and one from Western National. In addition, a rival city tour was provided by Ryans Coaches and among its mixed fleet of vehicles was an ex-South Midland Series 2 VRT and an ex-Southdown (Brighton & Hove) VRT3.

Conversion to open-top often extends the life of a vehicle. Alongside the VRTs in Bath, Badgerline has operated a 1941 Bristol/ECW K-type open-topper while an even older 1939 K5G has regularly run on the Isle of Wight with Bristol LDs and the VRT open-toppers of Southern Vectis. It is very likely that many open-top VRTs will remain active well into the future, with inland tours and those operations which continue throughout the winter becoming ever more popular. And the first Wednesday in June each year sees open-top buses of all types – including VRTs – make the annual 'pilgrimage' to Epsom Downs for the Derby, where the long-standing tradition of such vehicles acting as grandstands alongside the racecourse, seems to compel their attendance at this event!

With such a buoyant open-top bus business in Britain, the role of the open-top VR seems assured for many years to come.

Right:
Demonstrating that the tops of convertible VRTs really are detachable is Badgerline 8607, about to have its roof replaced for a winter season. UFX 859S was among those new to Hants & Dorset before passing to Southern Vectis. In 1983 it (and sister UFX 860S) became involved in a further exchange for a pair of standard VRTs between Southern Vectis and Bristol Omnibus, moving to Bath in 1984. Unfortunately, this bus was damaged beyond repair by fire in December 1992 as a result of a welding accident. *M. S. Curtis*

8

On the Road

When the VR first appeared, comparisons were inevitably made with Bristol's front-engined, Lodekka double-deck model, and also with the by-then established rear-engined Leyland Atlantean and Daimler Fleetline chassis. In fact the VR was, in many respects, unlike any of these vehicles, and from a driving and passenger viewpoint represented a number of departures from previous practice.

Among the first to drive the VR prototypes, in both chassis and bodied form, was Mr A. Alan Townsin, in his capacity as correspondent for the journal *Bus & Coach*. Alan Townsin reported the VR to be 'a most promising newcomer' and found the controls both smooth and responsive, while the driving position was praised for its comfort. (It should be remembered that the prototypes featured an inclined steering wheel, unlike the more upright steering position within a shorter cab on later, production models.) Two rear axle ratios were available, 4.23 to 1 or 4.89 to 1, linked to either a four- or five-speed gearbox. Initially, top speeds of between 45mph and 52mph could be achieved by these combinations while retaining generous hill-climbing abilities. Pendant-type foot pedals were used for both accelerator and braking systems, and while the footbrake produced no unusual characteristics for an air braking system, the accelerator required considerable effort.

From the passengers' point of view, initially the changes from previous Bristol models were minimal, with ECW's familiar and restrained styling adapted to suit the VR chassis, although the small step inside the entrance was a disappointment after Bristol and ECW had so cleverly achieved completely stepless floors in the F-series Lodekkas. However, the novelty of passing the driver upon boarding was something most Tilling company passengers had not encountered before on a double-decker. Of course, it was this arrangement which would enable production VRs to be worked as one-man operated (OMO) vehicles (sex equality had yet to influence the adoption of the term one-*person* operated), and made possible the progressive withdrawal of conductors on many services. In such circumstances the fitting of a periscope allowed the top deck to be viewed from the driver's cab. The VR was therefore often to be associated with conversions of routes from crew to driver-only operation, which not only produced economies but also alleviated the chronic staff shortages experienced by many operators in the 1960s and 1970s.

It will be recalled that the two bodied VRX prototypes were eventually sold to the Bristol Omnibus Co, and while in its ownership (during August 1972) the author journeyed on HHW 933D from Weston-super-Mare to Bristol. This vehicle was fully laden and, whilst smooth running occurred at high speeds, an uncomfortably high-pitched transmission whine developed as speed increased. When a gradient was encountered power was lost while considerable juddering and vibration was apparent as gear changes were made at low speeds.

Right:
Whilst the Bristol VR was a very stable vehicle, it was a matter of regret that its leaf-spring suspension was never updated and replaced by air suspension. With its weight thrown here on to the front axle, Western National 1071, a Series 2 VRT/SL, attempts to re-enter the main flow of traffic at Newquay. *M. S. Curtis*

A month later a rare opportunity arose to ride on sister vehicle GGM 431D while it spent a day operating on Bristol City service 13 between Staple Hill and Bedminster. On this occasion the ride was faultless, with smooth operation at all times in all conditions.

Although both VRX prototypes spent lengthy periods out of use, as is sometimes the case with experimental or non-standard vehicles – especially in large fleets – one always had the impression that GGM 431D presented the fewer problems of the two. This certainly seemed to be the case while operating in Bristol, and ultimately may explain why it survived longer than its twin.

The production VRL coaches used for long distance motorway services by W.C. Standerwick were altogether different machines! Operated principally from Standerwick's Blackpool depot, these too experienced mechanical difficulties on occasion but generally, when engaged on the high-speed operations for which they were built, their performance was spectacular. Passengers, particularly those on the upper deck, would hardly notice the engine start up, and on tickover it was almost impossible to hear the engine running inside the vehicle. The remoteness of both engine and gearbox was to lead to problems, as the driver was much less aware of what was happening at the rear than on a vehicle with the engine at the front or amidships. Indeed, in this respect the VRLs compared unfavourably even with a VRT, since at least the latter's engine was audible from the cab.

The VRLs were therefore not without their engineering problems which, when they arose, were invariably associated with the drive-line and transmission. Moreover, if a serious breakdown occurred there was the added problem of finding replacement coaches as two conventional vehicles were needed to cater for a full complement of VRL passengers and their luggage! As an aside, it may be significant that the author, who regularly observed Bristols in chassis form on test or on their delivery run to the bodybuilder, can only once ever remember seeing a Bristol chassis broken down at the roadside – and this was a VRL destined for Standerwick!

Nevertheless, when running properly, Standerwick's VRL coaches were extremely impressive. They were powerful, offering high standards of passenger comfort. Of particular significance was their ability to race along the new motorways, having a high cruising speed which comfortably matched or exceeded most other motorised traffic then on Britain's roads. Unfortunately, their role as front-line express coaches was relatively short and these vehicles never seemed at ease on slower, tourist sightseeing or private hire work. Upon demotion to such duties, they rapidly faded from prominence and few survived long in regular service.

The VRT model presented rather fewer problems, and the improvements progressively introduced during the lengthy production runs overcame many of the difficulties found in the earliest versions. In 1969 both *Bus & Coach* and *Motor Transport* published the results of a

Above left:
The 30 Standerwick Bristol VRL/LH double-deck coaches offered breathtaking performance and cruised past other traffic with ease on the motorways between London and the Northwest, in an era when many family saloon cars were not built for sustained, high-speed driving. Here No 70, destined for Blackpool, is captured at high speed on the M6 near Manchester. Were Britain's motorways really once as quiet as this? *M. S. Curtis*

Above right:
The ability to produce the Bristol VR with lowheight bodywork was crucial for many operators. In wet conditions a VRT/SL with ECW 13ft 8in-tall 'standard' lowheight bodywork passes below the bridge at Bitton station (carrying the Avon Valley Railway) which has a height clearance of 14ft 3in. *M. S. Curtis*

detailed road test of an early VRT/SL (which formed part of the Western SMT order), once again undertaken by A. Alan Townsin. It included performance trials at the MIRA (Motor Industry Research Association) proving ground at Lindley, near Nuneaton.

The vehicle in question was of course ECW-bodied, powered by a Gardner 6LXB engine down rated to 165bhp at 1,700rpm. Tests were conducted with added weights to represent a full passenger load, although an unladen weight of around 8 tons 16 cwt (8,970kg) was recorded, which was to remain little changed throughout the various production series of VRT/SLs with ECW coachwork. A top speed of 42mph was achieved on the test bus, although a range of four different rear axle ratios was available throughout the production life of the VRT. These could affect this performance considerably, with a maximum of 54mph being possible with the earliest VRTs. Specifications generally varied in line with expected use, ranging from regular stop-start urban operations to longer-distance, limited-stop services requiring higher speeds.

The road test showed fuel consumption ranged between 7.95mpg and 13.6mpg on simulated service journeys, with even better results possible by steady cruising. Indeed, some operators of Gardner-engined VRTs regularly achieved average fuel consumption well in excess of 10mpg, which by any standards was good and considerably more economical than other (including later) rival models. This clearly signified that the operational costs of a VRT compared most favourably with 36ft long single-deckers, yet offered the added advantages of a shorter overall length with great manoeuvrability, plus a much higher seating capacity.

From the driver's viewpoint, the VRT offered greatly improved performance compared with earlier Bristol double-deckers. This was especially appreciated when hill-climbing or pulling away in traffic, and allowed the VRT to keep pace with other vehicles more successfully than had been usual for heavy vehicles in the 1960s. Gear changing was effortless with a semi-automatic box, but easily abused – and if a driver failed to pause correctly or listen to engine revs during changes, jerking and snatching resulted, culminating not only in an uncomfortable ride for passengers but also costly damage to the transmission. It was this problem which persuaded many operators to experiment with fully-automatic control.

The VR cab was of the single-piece glass fibre moulded type with easily understood instruments and very clear warning display to the driver's left, in front of the small gear-change control attached to the side of the steering column. The spring parking brake and door controls were arranged to the right of the driver.

The Bristol VRT's road holding was excellent, but the decision to introduce a more upright steering position was regrettable, and the steering, without power assistance, could be heavy. At slow speeds with a well-loaded bus, steering could be *so* heavy that it led to disputes between management and driving staff in at least three West of England companies. On early VRs, the accelerator too required considerable effort both to depress and hold in position (in contrast to earlier Bristol designs), but with the later introduction of an air-operated throttle, such criticism was eliminated. However, the arrangement involving a small floor-mounted heel rest for the driver's right foot to assist in pedal operation always appeared to be a cumbersome afterthought and spoiled what was otherwise a well thought-out cab design.

The author had first-hand operating experience of all three series of Bristol VRT and encountered some of the disagreements involving VRs with heavy steering, which occurred with vehicles of Bristol Omnibus, Western National and Southern National. At Bristol, the troubles (which were much publicised in the local press) centred largely around vehicles employed on Bristol City services in the late 1970s. They were resolved, following the refusal by drivers to operate VRs without power steering, by an agreement to fit power steering progressively throughout the entire VRT fleet. Within Western National, non-power steering VRs would not be allocated to all-day workings at some depots, being confined instead to peak-hour and contract duties, while in the 1980s Southern National was among many companies across the country which attempted to deal with some of the worst offending buses by fitting a non-standard power steering system called Auto-Steer. This necessitated raising the driving position and featured a curious characteristic of power assistance cutting-in, sometimes unexpectedly, which in turn was not without its own problems. The standard power steering arrangement for the Bristol VR was superb, offering positive handling with little effort, and cured the steering problems once and for all.

Brakes on Bristol VRTs were excellent, indeed application in normal conditions had to be made with care as the air system was capable of stopping a VR very abruptly, which could unbalance unsuspecting standing passengers. In normal circumstances the system provided a very effective but smooth brake application.

A feature of the VR familiar to drivers, passengers and particularly pedestrians was the air pressure release valve which expelled air periodically as pressure built up beyond required levels. This produced a 'wooshing' sound from time to time, which of course was completely beyond the driver's control. On one occasion, in a quiet rural setting near Weston-super-Mare, the writer watched a horse with lady rider being carefully overtaken by a VR. At that moment air pressure was released, startling the horse; and while the rider struggled to maintain control she chastised a bewildered driver who was far from certain what it was he had done wrong!

Of course, each VRT, like most Bristol models, was initially driven in chassis form: first, in order to test the vehicle, then on the delivery run to the body builder, which in the vast majority of cases involved the 236-mile journey from Bristol to Lowestoft. Mike Walker, writing in *Bristol Passenger* magazine for August 1981, described how handling a VRT chassis was very different from driving a finished bus. Wearing a crash helmet, the driver sat on a temporary wooden seat (and cushion). With only an offside driving mirror, manoeuvres involved a glance over the shoulder to judge clearances as the whole frame could be viewed from the driving position, whilst the use of hand signals was another necessity.

Without the weight of bodywork, the chassis flexed and twisted and seemed considerably more powerful, while the driver, perched in his temporary cab, felt extremely vulnerable without the protection of coachwork. Brakes and steering had to be treated with far more respect as the only significant weight was provided by the power pack at the rear. And while a suitably adjusted driving technique could compensate for these differences, the lack of rigidity of the chassis was impossible to avoid and uneven road surfaces caused the driver to be shaken and tossed as the frame distorted.

One can only admire the regular chassis drivers who tirelessly endured these conditions, through all seasons and weather conditions, to ensure supplies of new chassis continued to reach their destination safely.

Returning to the completed vehicles, VRT travel for passengers was generally an agreeable experience, the improved performance over earlier models inevitably causing those on board to be impressed. The VRT was very stable, even when driven through tight manoeuvres at speed – which was well within its capabilities – but the front overhang resulted in rather more bounce and roll for front upper-deck passengers than would be found on a front-engined bus. Downstairs, the leaf springs sometimes creaked, which was a further irritation, and surprisingly these were never replaced with air suspension, especially when one remembers Bristol included pneumatic suspension in many of its other designs, before and after the VRT.

The seating layout of ECW models has already been commented on. While the seats themselves were very comfortable, the ECW seating arrangement for dual-door VRTs (with centre stairs) left much to be desired. This did not deter a reporter from BBC Radio Bristol, who boarded such a vehicle to record a report on their first day of regular operation in Bristol in July 1972. One suspects he was either an infrequent bus traveller or had prepared his account before inspecting the interior, as his introduction began, 'I'm travelling on one of the most comfortable buses I've ever been on, and it should be for £11,000...'. Despite the brightly painted exteriors of the Bristol Omnibus examples, many passengers were less satisfied with the raised seats and awkward stairs of the dual-door ECW bodywork. Yet these were difficulties not found for example in Reading, where the two-door VRT/LLs carried Northern Counties bodies which featured a straight staircase; and single-door bodies by various coachbuilders (of the style carried by the majority of VRTs) presented few problems for

Right:
Engine accessibility was good on all VR models. This VRT3 demonstrates the ease with which inspection of major units could be achieved without compromising engine compartment encapsulation. Side panels were vertically hinged, and while the upper rear section was also hinged at the top, the lower panel was completely removable. The engine in this instance is a Gardner 6LXB unit, with gearbox positioned on the right, below the substantial air-inlet ducting. *M. S. Curtis*

their passengers, who appreciated the comfortable and attractive interior and convenient seating layouts.

Although it was not as piercing as on prototype HHW 933D, VRTs cruising at high speed produced the characteristic transmission whine (shared with Bristol's RE single-deck chassis) which was audible both inside and outside the vehicle – but was by no means unpleasant. Indeed, on occasions this sound conveyed an impression of speed and efficient running.

For bus engineers, the Bristol VRT was initially seen as a substantial departure from the traditional Bristol approach and was not regarded as performing as reliably or satisfactorily as the previous generations of Bristol double-deckers. Rear-engined models certainly demanded more attention than vehicles of traditional layout, and as already described, this dissatisfaction was too much for the Scottish operators to bear during the early VR years. But, gradually, design improvement followed design improvement and weaknesses in transmission and structure were overcome, such that by the late 1980s the VRT had become a well-respected, dependable model, with even early examples giving good service at many locations.

Among the few detectable faults which remained apparent on many VRTs was the need to strengthen the rear corner section of the body immediately above the engine. Some engineers considered the sound deadening achieved by engine encapsulation on VRT3s to be an encumbrance, so removed the baffle plates below the engine (which naturally increased noise!), although there are certainly VRT3s which continue to retain undertrays beneath the engine. Also, Leyland 500-series engined VRTs were always noiser (both internally and externally) and livelier than Gardner-engined versions, while those fitted with Leyland 0.680 units near the end of VRT production produced a deep, throaty roar which was amplified through the engine's ventilation ducting.

Nevertheless, Bristol VRs continue to give economical and reliable service with vast numbers still active across Britain. Although second-hand examples find a ready market, many remain with their original owners – or direct successors. And while some of the newer generations of double-deckers are themselves destined for long lives and are highly regarded, the Bristol VRT continues to attract praise in many quarters, with perhaps only the lack of air suspension letting the design down when running alongside newer models. Even so, in other respects – including performance, noise, exhaust emission levels and floor heights – it maintains very acceptable standards more than 25 years after its design was first unveiled.

Right:
The interior of ECW's dual-door, centre staircase bodywork for VRT/SLs was cluttered and disorganised. This view, looking forward on the lower deck, illustrates how the seats (which in this case have vinyl coverings) are arranged at different levels, including side facing over all four wheel arches. The sharply turning staircase and centre exit partitions complicate what would otherwise be an open saloon. *M. S. Curtis*

9

The Successors

Following the appearance of the Leyland National single-decker in 1970, speculation mounted regarding the introduction of an equivalent double-deck model which might act as a replacement for the Leyland group's existing range of double-deckers, viz the Atlantean, Fleetline and Bristol VRT.

By early 1973, it was clear that plans were at an advanced stage for the development of such a bus that, like the Leyland National saloon, would include a turbo-charged power unit and be of integral construction. In the spring of that year a chassis and engine unit had been completed for trials, and a full size mock-up revealed. A totally enclosed rear, transverse engine was to be incorporated into the design with the radiator mounted above, while self-levelling suspension was another feature. Power-assisted steering and a choice of fully or semi-automatic transmission was proposed with a new design of control system offering smoother gear changes. At this stage, the new model had yet to receive a name but the design had been developed by Leyland under the title 'Project B15'.

Further details of this design were published in the autumn of 1974, by which time the VRT3 chassis had, of course, just been unveiled. This assured the future of Bristol's double-decker since it was now clear that the B15, rather than threatening future VRT production, would complement it. The Bristol model would continue as a lowheight model while the B15 would provide the basis of a new generation of sophisticated double-deckers intended primarily to satisfy the demands of customers operating in the larger conurbations. Production of B15 at a body-builder, such as Park Royal Vehicles or C. H. Roe, was also anticipated, and it was confirmed that the 500-series fixed-head engine and new Hydracyclic transmission would be included. Leyland – having undertaken a great deal of design and development work – was pinning its hopes on the B15 design after witnessing a major return of support among operators for double-deckers.

A B15 prototype was ready for service trials in London by November 1975 – its operation in the capital being extremely significant since its design had evolved to adhere closely to London Transport's requirements. It was viewed by some commentators as a further development of the still-born FRM rear-engined Routemaster bus of the 1960s, immediately conjuring images of very high design standards but levels of sophistication and complexity which might not be desired by many provincial customers.

The integral monocoque construction, independent front suspension, power-hydraulic brakes and suspended 501 engine were among the B15's advanced features, and, in an attempt to share production responsibility (as it had with NBC for the Leyland National), Leyland invited operators such as London Transport and the Passenger Transport Executives to join a manufacturing con-

Right:
March 1976, and a new generation of Leyland double-decker was captured on film undergoing trials with London Transport, in Buckingham Palace Road, Victoria. This is B15 prototype 04, registered NHG 732P, which at the time had still to enter passenger-carrying service. *M. S. Curtis*

Below right:
Displaying an intriguing combination of Bristol VR and B15/Titan styling is Bristol/ECW prototype B45-01, forerunner of Bristol's next generation of double-decker which became known as the Olympian. B45-01 was built in 1979 and spent four years as a test rig before joining Stevensons of Uttoxeter, which by then already operated the last VRT. It is seen on a Rugeley local service in 1989, carrying registration Q246 FVT.
M. S. Curtis

sortium – but without success. Nevertheless, in July 1977 it was announced that Leyland would proceed alone with production of the model, which would now be powered by Leyland's TL11 or Gardner engines, and would revive the name of an earlier, popular Leyland double-decker to become the Titan TN15. Production was to begin at Leyland, with body structures produced by Park Royal; and there were plans for later production to be transferred to AEC, once again reflecting the London emphasis. Unfortunately, proposals for future assembly of the Titan were to run less than smoothly, and expected orders from major operators outside London were either disappointing, or failed to materialise at all.

Meanwhile, a separate scheme for a new lowheight double-decker, which could eventually replace the Bristol VRT, had already received considerable attention. As early as February 1977, rumours had been circulating within the industry that a new chassis, incorporating B15 parts and suitable for receiving separate bodywork, was being evaluated. By the time B15 had been launched as the Titan, a project was in hand to build a lowheight, body-on-chassis version of this model. A year later it was known that the new lowheight chassis would be known as the B45 and that much of the development work was actually being undertaken at Bristol.

By late 1979 the first B45 chassis had been sent from Bristol Commercial Vehicles to Lowestoft. There it received an ECW lowheight, two-door body shell which, in many respects, resembled the Titan and was very much squarer than traditional ECW styles. However, it did receive a VRT3 dash panel, grille and windscreen so as it approached it appeared at first glance, to be a VR! Its appearance from the rear also followed the VRT pattern with enclosed engine, flush lower-deck rear window (unlike Titan's offset, recessed rear saloon glazing) and engine ventilation grilles above the waistband, but all to a much less rounded style than had previously been associated with ECW products. This vehicle, which was devoid of interior fittings, was painted red and became a test rig until 1983, when it lost its centre door, received seating and interior trim and, eventually, entered revenue earning service with Stevensons of Uttoxeter registered Q246 FVT.

Unfortunately, Titan production was meanwhile encountering serious difficulties. Since 1978, Titan assembly had been based at the Park Royal coachworks (AEC having closed in May 1979). Although orders for 800 Titans had been received, placed almost entirely by London Transport and the PTEs, fewer than 100 had been produced by September 1979. It was then disclosed that Park Royal Vehicles was also to close – ownership of both PRV and C.H. Roe of Leeds having recently been transferred to Bus Manufacturers (Holdings) Ltd, joining Bristol, ECW and the Leyland National plant at Workington under this jointly-controlled Leyland/NBC organisation.

Despite this, it was never intended to cease production of the Titan since Leyland planned to transfer manufacture to another plant, where output would not only continue, but increase. The risk of losing some Titan orders during this transitional period was nevertheless accepted; and, as both Atlantean and Fleetline had remained available throughout this period, production of these chassis was actually stepped up to satisfy the shortfall of new double-deckers while a new home was sought for Titan assembly.

After a short period of uncertainty, Leyland announced that it hoped to see Titan production uninterrupted, with continuity of supplies to customers (and in particular London Transport) achieved by producing underframes at the Workington Leyland National plant, with bodywork added by ECW at Lowestoft. Since running units were attached directly to the body structure at Park Royal, some design changes would be needed in order to achieve this, as separate underframes would have to be built in Cumbria before bodywork was added 325 miles away in Suffolk. However, this proposal produced the interesting prospect of ECW building, side-by-side, bodies for both Titans and the majority of B45s produced in Bristol.

As these plans were published, ECW (whose main output continued to be bodies for Bristol VRTs) was completing bodywork on the second B45 prototype chassis. This was finished to full standards and painted in NBC red livery for Ribble (later receiving fleet No 2100). Its overall appearance was very similar to the first B45, except it carried a single-door body, and while the VRT-style windscreen was retained, gone was the VRT dash panel, replaced by a new design of dash and grille which bore a strong family resemblance to the Titan. While they may have looked similar, the B45 had a conventional chassis and was suitable for both highbridge or lowheight bodywork, whereas the Titan remained available only as an integral highbridge bus. Moreover, though many of the running units were common (including the whole of the power pack), this was of less significance to the bodybuilder. What was significant was the high number of unskilled staff needed to build the Titan.

The move to transfer Titan production to Lowestoft would have involved a major factory extension and the recruitment of some 300 additional unskilled and semi-skilled employees. ECW already employed 900 staff, 500 of whom were highly skilled and wanted their skills to be protected. Accordingly, there was considerable concern over this issue, to the extent that ECW's existing work-force could not be persuaded to accept expanded production using unskilled staff. By the beginning of February 1980, only six weeks after Leyland revealed its plans for ECW, the ECW staff had voted to reject Leyland's proposals for Titan assembly at Lowestoft. Perhaps they were mindful that Titan had brought about the demise of Park Royal, although a different attitude may also have existed since ECW staff, like those at Bristol, were proud of their skillls and loyal to the factory in which they worked – and which they feared might be threatened by new assembly methods.

In retrospect their decision for the immediate future may have been correct, for it was the much simpler B45, not the sophisticated Titan, which was attracting more and more attention. Nevertheless, while the Titan was again without a production base, there was little prospect of maintaining deliveries without interruption.

By March 1980 it had been decided that Workington would be responsible for the complete assembly of Titans in future, but delays would cause a serious break in production from mid-1980 until well into 1981. Outside London, the Titan attracted little support, with small batches joining Greater Manchester and West Midlands PTEs. Reading became the only municipal customer with a dozen examples, while London Transport bought over 1,100. The last of these was delivered in 1984 after which there was an absence of further orders from London – and production of the Titan ceased completely.

The B45 was to do far better. The first public viewing of the B45 occurred, unusually, on BBC television in a programme from *The Risk Business* series featuring the bus-building industry, which was broadcast during May 1980, and shots of both prototypes were seen. Shortly afterwards, the first photograph to be published of a B45 appeared in the June 1980 issue of NBC's *Bus News* staff newspaper. It depicted the second prototype at Preston bus station, displaying registration UHV 995V, although it was later licensed as DBV 100W.

Bristol's B45 could now be studied in more depth, with both chassis and body incorporating an intriguing combination of Bristol-ECW and Leyland design and styling. Following the two prototypes which had been rigorously tested, a further seven pre-production B45s had been built by Bristol by September 1980. These were to continue a painstaking test programme, ensuring that there was no repeat of the failure to test the VRT before production commenced.

More details of the design were released in October of that year, in time for the Motor Show at the National Exhibition Centre, where no fewer than five B45s were displayed (against one Titan). These comprised a left-hand drive chassis and an ECW-bodied example in Alexander (Midland) livery, on the Leyland Vehicles stand; two Alexander-bodied examples, for Strathclyde PTE and a long-wheelbase overseas demonstrator; and a Greater Manchester vehicle on Northern Counties' stand. A name for the B45 was also revealed – it was to be the Olympian.

The name 'Olympian' was to be used in conjunction with the 'Leyland' name despite its manufacturer, Bristol Commercial Vehicles (which continued in any case to refer to this model as the B45) remaining under joint Leyland/National Bus Co ownership through Bus Manufacturers Ltd. Nevertheless, most of the earlier Olympians built by Bristol were actually licensed as 'Bristols' rather than 'Leylands'.

The Olympian chassis was constructed with perimeter framing, not unlike that seen some years earlier on Lodekkas and VRLs, and was constructed in three modules. The rear section contained a dropped-centre rear axle (perpetuating the Lodekka concept), semi- or fully-automatic gearbox with Hydracyclic transmission taken from the Titan, and a suspended engine arrangement, which overcame many of the structural stress-related difficulties of VRTs, Atlanteans and Fleetlines – with engine supports below the power unit. Initially, Leyland's turbo-charged TL11 engine developing 170bhp at 1850rpm or Gardner's naturally aspirated 6LXB producing 177bhp at 1850rpm were offered, the latter remaining popular with NBC operators, among others.

The front module contained an excellent ergonomically-designed Leyland National/Titan style cab, a front-mounted radiator (following Bristol practice), and front axle. Between them was the centre module, which consisted of the frame between the axles. In standard form this produced a bus of 9.5m (31ft 5in) overall length, equivalent to a VRT/SL. However, larger centre sections could be fitted as alternatives to extend overall length (and wheelbase) to produce 10.3m, 11.2m and 12m long models, including three-axle variants if required, offering tremendous versatility. All-round air suspension ensured a smooth and stable ride which was a great improvement on the VRT's leaf springs. However, like the Bristol VR, Olympians had split

Right:
Production Olympians with ECW bodywork featured a revised grille not unlike that fitted to Titans. This is Devon General 1814 (A686 KDV), an ONLXB/1R model which was the last bus ever built by Bristol Commercial Vehicles. It is viewed in Exeter High Street in December 1983, having just entered service. *M. S. Curtis*

dual-circuit air-braking, and a spring parking brake.

Production of Olympian chassis commenced at Brislington early in 1981 and, by the end of August of that year, had completely replaced the VRT. Naturally, with the Bristol/ECW/Gardner combination, it became the VRT's obvious successor for National Bus fleets and by the end of the year East Midland, Eastern National, Northern General, Ribble, United Counties and Yorkshire Traction had received examples. Scottish operators also instantly took to the Olympian, with Alexander (Northern), Lothian and Strathclyde PTE becoming operators of the type in the same period, while among the English PTEs, Greater Manchester, Merseyside and West Yorkshire ordered some of the earliest Olympians, together with the municipalities of Bournemouth, Cardiff and Derby.

Perhaps of even greater significance was the overseas interest in the model. Several early Olympians were exported, including left-hand drive versions, and the first three-axle chassis with uprated TL11 engine was built for Kowloon Motor Bus of Hong Kong, shortly after VRT production had ceased.

Bodywork of both highbridge and lowheight configuration was found on Olympians from the start. The widespread interest from all sectors of the industry was reflected in a greater variety of bodybuilders

Right:
Bristol built versions of the B45 Olympian in various lengths to suit customers' requirements. This 11.2m (36ft 7in) long coach (ADD 50Y), fitted with ECW bodywork, was reminiscent of the Standerwick VRL double-deck coaches, although having a longer 6.5m (21ft 5in) wheelbase than the VRL/LHs. When new, it was finished in white National Express livery but later passed to Bristol Omnibus to become one of the first vehicles painted in Badgerline colours, as shown. *M. S. Curtis*

working on its chassis than Bristol had seen since the 1940s, including Alexander, East Lancs, Marshall and Northern Counties. ECW remained the most important coachbuilder, of course, but the Leyland group's other bodybuilder, Roe (whose body designs looked generally very like those of ECW but were surprisingly different in detail) became an important builder of normal-height Olympian bodies, mainly for non-NBC customers – although Bristol and London Country were recipients of Roe Olympians to ease pressure on ECW. In general, UK bus production was in decline, but Olympian output was running at such healthy levels that the future for Bristol Commercial Vehicles and ECW seemed assured. However this was not to be.

Its role as partner in the jointly-owned bus-building concerns appeared to be an increasing burden for the National Bus Company. In Tilling days, the operating departments had strongly influenced designs from Bristol and ECW, and elsewhere it was possible to see operators exerting enormous influence over vehicle design – whether giants like London Transport or smaller, local authorities whose fleets nevertheless displayed a distinct individuality by the look or layout of their vehicles. While it was certainly involved in projects such as the Leyland National, NBC was perhaps less influential than might have been expected, often appearing content for Leyland to dominate the vehicle-building partnership. Arguably, National Bus failed on occasions to guide, sufficiently strongly, its manufacturers to construct vehicles based on its needs and experience. It therefore earned itself a reputation for forcing some models – in particular the Leyland National – on to operating companies that might have preferred entirely different buses! The potential for NBC to have adopted a more forceful position in manufacturing was considerable, and it was a pity this opportunity seemed to be missed. In the case of the Olympian, however, its designers drew on comment and experience from a wide range of operating companies, not just those in NBC, to produce a rear-engined double-decker which was exactly what was wanted, and which would succeed for this reason alone.

In November 1982, NBC decided it no longer wanted to be directly involved in bus manufacturing. It therefore sold its share of Bus Manufacturers (Holdings) Ltd, including Bristol Commercial Vehicles, Eastern Coach Works, Leyland National and C.H. Roe, to Leyland Vehicles Ltd, which had been managing the factories from day-to-day for some years. The previous year the bus manufacturing plants had, unusually, made a loss, and, officially at least, NBC stated it was for this reason that it had allowed Leyland to take complete control. Neither orders nor production of the Olympian was expected to be unduly influenced by the new arrangement.

The high quality of Bristol chassis construction, and still more Olympian interest, boded well for the future. The first 11.2m long coach version, recalling the VRL coaches, entered service in 1982 on National Express services with Wessex, based in Bristol. However, a

Right:
Comparative trials were undertaken in London prior to the purchase of large numbers of new vehicles for the capital in the mid-1980s. Among the vehicles evaluated (which included Leyland Olympians) was this front-engined Volvo Ailsa B55, fleet No V3 (A103 SUU) which evoked memories of the South African Bristol VRLs, since its Alexander bodywork incorporated a similar stairs and doorway arrangement. Unfortunately, it saw little service in this form and is posed here at Stockwell during March 1985. *M. S. Curtis*

slump in orders for new vehicles continued to plague other plants in the Leyland organisation, especially Workington where there had been a dramatic fall in demand for the Leyland National, while Bristol had seen significant investment in recent years. By the end of 1982 some 500 Olympians had been produced and orders remained at healthy levels. Then came disaster for Bristol! In January 1983, just two months after Leyland had acquired complete control of the works, it was announced that Bristol Commercial Vehicles would be closed later that year. This stunned everyone involved in Bristol production.

The last Bristol-built chassis, No ON995, which became Devon General 1814 (A686 KDV), was finished at the end of September 1983. Including the prototype and pre-production B45s, a total of 1,004 B45/Olympians had been built at Bristol, but the end had come for BCV after 75 years of bus building, and new models from the home of such famous chassis as the 4-tonner, the Lodekka, the RE and VR would never emerge again. However, the Olympian was not to die.

Such had been the decline in bus production generally, caused to a substantial degree by the phasing out of new bus grants, that spare capacity existed elsewhere. Olympian chassis production was therefore transferred to the Workington factory (alongside Titans), with Olympian parts manufactured at Leyland.

There was no break in Olympian production, with some of the first Workington Olympians using frames already assembled by Bristol, while one chassis was sent to Workington after completion by Bristol, to be dismantled and reassembled for familiarisation purposes. Some minor design changes occurred during the transfer of production. A nuance of Olympian production detail was, for example, the position of the rear water filler cap. This was on the near side (as it was on VRT3s) only on Bristol-built Olympians, together with the very first Workington examples, and it acts as a recognition point! ECW-bodied examples (but not Roe ones) also displayed slightly larger 'Leyland' grille badges from the change – which may not be a universal item of minutiae but displayed great subtlety on the part of somebody at Lowestoft!

The Olympian continued, with another thousand built during the next three years, some now with Voith gearboxes, but more trauma was in store for the Leyland organisation. A year after the closure of Bristol, came the demise of Chas H. Roe's works in Leeds: except it didn't quite disappear. The following year the works was reopened by a number of former Roe employees to become Optare, and among its new body range was a continuation of the double-deck bodywork for Olympians. A year later (by which time Olympian production had moved yet again to Farington, near the town of Leyland!) there came another blow. Under the terms of a management buy-out of Leyland Bus, Eastern Coach Works was to close, and by early 1987 ECW's last new bodies had been completed, its final orders including one from London Buses (as London Transport buses had become) for bodywork on 260 new Olympians. After the closure of Bristol, it was almost inevitable that ECW would eventually follow, with Leyland's own bodybuilding concentrated on Workington, the newest plant, which was still far from fully utilised. The intention was to transfer the ECW design of Olympian body to the Leyland National factory but this took a considerable time, and it was not until July 1988 that the first Workington highbridge-bodied Olympians were delivered (for use on the Isle of Man) and almost a year later before the lowheight version entered production. Both Optare and Northern Counties therefore gained a number of additional orders during these months!

Returning to 1984, London Regional Transport embarked on comparative trials of various buses before selecting ECW-bodied Leyland Olympians for its next major batch of double-deckers. It was intended that a dozen experimental vehicles would run on route 170 from Roehampton, through Central London to Aldwych, including three Leyland Olympians with various combinations of engine and transmission. Also included were three Dennis Dominators, three front-engined Volvo Ailsa B55s and MCW Metrobus MK IIs. Perhaps the most interesting of these vehicles was one of the Volvos: V3 (A103 SUU), which had Alexander bodywork with dual doors, but unlike others in the trial it had passenger doors at the extreme front and rear, the latter behind the rear axle. Two staircases were also incorporated on the offside, one in the conventional position over the front offside wheel, while another was positioned Routemaster-style, opposite the rear door. Such a layout was reminiscent of the South African Bristol VRLs and was precisely one of the layouts envisaged by Bristol designers for the home market when conceiving the VRL design. Unfortunately, as with the Bristol design 20 years before, a production run of Volvos to this pattern was not forthcoming.

Olympian production reverted to Workington once more during 1990. The Cummins L10 power unit coupled to ZF automatic transmission had largely replaced the original Gardner/Hydracyclic combination, although Gardner engines remained an option. The extraordinary degree to which production locations had been changed also gave the Olympian the dubious distinction of becoming one of the least settled motor vehicle designs ever! And Leyland's difficulties were far from over, with the uncertainty following the 1985 Transport Act causing new bus orders in general to remain low. Two years earlier, in 1988, Leyland's bus-building business had been acquired by Volvo and in December 1991 Volvo announced it would be closing Workington, the Leyland group's last bastion of bus manufacturing, and cease involvement in bodybuilding altogether. This represented something of an irony, with Leyland having itself swallowed so many of Britain's successful bus chassis and body manufacturers.

But the Olympian – by now a seasoned survivor – was to relocate once again, this time to Volvo's Irvine plant in Scotland! It was here that it was again modified and updated, and with Volvo's own 9.6-litre engine as standard, was re-launched as the 'Volvo' Olympian in March 1993.

Thus the Bristol VRT's direct successor, the B45 Olympian, entered a new chapter in its history – and it remains the most popular of all the current double-deck designs. Its capacity to survive in the most trying of circumstances for the bus manufacturing industry reflects its sound design and extensive testing by Bristol and Leyland in the late 1970s and early 1980s. Despite the changes in ownership and production base, it continues the basic concept of the Leyland Atlantean, Daimler Fleetline and of course Bristol VRT, to provide one of the most efficient methods of moving in excess of 70 people on our roads.

Right:
From March 1993 a modified Volvo Olympian entered production at Volvo's Irvine factory in Scotland. Among the first to enter service (during summer 1993) was Western National 801 (K801 ORL), a Northern Counties-bodied example, arriving here at Paignton amid a selection of Bayline minibuses. Ten years earlier Olympians had been built by Bristol, and the model continues as the direct successor to the Bristol VRT.
M. S. Curtis

10

VRs in Trouble

Since their introduction, Bristol VRs have safely operated many millions of miles each year – and continue to do so. Whilst there is most certainly no suggestion that VRs are more accident prone than other vehicles of their class, inevitably occasions arise where mishaps or difficulties occur, and sometimes more serious incidents, involving VRs, have attracted attention. This serves as a sobering reminder that care is always needed on our roads.

When one reflects on the intensive work asked of these vehicles, it is remarkable that they have safely completed thousands of journeys each week for over 25 years, and it is a tribute to those responsible for their design, construction, maintenance and operation that they have done so. And it should not be forgotten that buses and coaches provide one of the safest forms of road travel, and the road passenger transport industry in general has an enviable safety record.

Right:
Western/Southern National regularly parked vehicles on railway property in Weymouth, supplementing its own garage parking facilities. One night in October 1986, No 559 (ATA 559L) was stolen from Weymouth station yard but the thief misjudged the position of the bus at the exit gate and crashed into a barrier. The bus was later repaired, but rebuilt to open-top form for sea-front use. *M. S. Curtis*

Right:
Weymouth once again, a few years earlier, and former Standerwick VRL No 60 (LRN 60J), by now in the ownership of Bangor City Football Club, arrives in the town for a match with the local team. Unfortunately the driver was not familiar with the town and, in error, turned his vehicle into a narrow residential street — through which it would not fit! Here it is being extracted across the Abbotsbury Road, with a little assistance from the local police. *M. S. Curtis*

Below:
Every bus operator's nightmare is a disaster of this sort. During July 1982 this National Welsh VRT/SL (No HR3978) was driven under a low bridge in Pontrhydyrun, near Cwmbran, while on an outing to Porthcawl. Six passengers died and eight others were injured. *Western Mail and Echo Ltd*

Right:
This was the scene on the morning of Wednesday, 14 July 1976 outside Trent's Meadow Road depot, Derby, where a major fire overnight had destroyed or seriously damaged over 40 vehicles. Surrounded by a variety of buses badly damaged in the blaze is a tangled mass of charred and twisted metal, all that remained of ECW-bodied VRT 793 (MAL 793P).
B. L. Jackson

Below:
Wilts & Dorset 3437 (GEL 687V), carrying an overall advert for an estate agent, nose-dived off the road across a pedestrian subway in Poole during the summer of 1992. A number of passengers were on board but miraculously no one was seriously injured. Reports at the time suggested that the driver collapsed at the wheel immediately before.
Evening Echo, Bournemouth

Right:
One of the most widely-publicised incidents involving a Bristol VRT occurred in Norwich during March 1988, when Eastern Counties VR266 (RAH 266W) found itself in a hole when a medieval chalk mine collapsed below the road. Nobody was hurt, however, and when recovered the bus was returned to service! *Eastern Daily Press, Norwich*

Below:
When things do go wrong, the ability to deal with the situation becomes a priority. City Line has an impressive fleet of recovery vehicles which includes this powerful Bedford breakdown truck, here providing a suspended tow to inoperative VRT/SL 5144 (AHU 521V) back to the garage for repairs. *M. S. Curtis*

11
Privatisation and Deregulation

Although changes such as the formation of the National Bus Company and the widespread adoption of one-person operation occurred during the production life of the Bristol VR, the British bus industry had, in comparison with what was to follow, been relatively stable throughout the 1960s and 1970s.

This situation was to change dramatically during the next decade as a result of the Transport Act 1985, and the Bristol VR would soon be plunged into the centre of a very different world so far as bus operation was concerned. The 1985 Act altered the structure, ownership and control of bus services throughout the country, yet, remarkably, and to a greater extent than many other passenger models, the Bristol VR survived. In many locations it strengthened its prominence by adapting to the new conditions, often running alongside very much smaller passenger vehicles.

Already, the idea of replacing conventional buses in urban areas with high frequency minibus services had been seen in the Southwest. During 1984 the wholesale conversion of services to minibus operation began in Exeter, while the first town network to be converted entirely to minibuses followed a year later at Weston-super-Mare. In the former case the operator was Devon General, while at Weston the minibuses were launched under the new Badgerline name – which at that time remained part of Bristol Omnibus. At both locations, Ford Transit vehicles were employed to replace various types of large buses, including Bristol VRs, and their arrival signalled the widespread introduction of minibus schemes throughout the National Bus Company, with some 3,000 minibuses added to NBC fleets in little more than three years! These included more Ford Transits, together with Freight Rover Sherpas and slightly larger types built by Iveco, Mercedes-Benz and Dodge-Renault.

The advantages of minibuses included the ability to offer higher frequency services and better penetration of peripheral housing estates, combined with lower running costs. With staff recruitment having become much less of a problem, these vehicles brushed aside their larger, conventional stable-mates in many locations.

With the phasing-out of bus grants for new vehicles and remaining funds taken up by large orders for minibuses, it is easy to understand why demand for large buses dropped drastically. In particular, Bristol had already ceased production in 1983, with ECW closing just over three years later. Other bus and coach builders also collapsed during these years, and many famous names disappeared from both the chassis and bodybuilding sectors of the bus manufacturing industry.

These events were largely a prelude to the main provisions of the new Transport Act, which would take effect from 1986. These would involve not only the privatisation of the National Bus Company but also the deregulation of local bus services outside London, allowing, for the first time since 1930, a return to on-street competition between operators. Suddenly, bus operation required a new commercial approach which, for most individuals within the bus industry, was a style not practised before. Gone were the network support grants and cross subsidies between services, and the relatively stable fabric of service networks was replaced by normal business principles of covering costs and providing profit. Some found this new environment exciting and challenging, while others were less enthusiastic. Although many bus companies have been successful, others have failed – with a few operators who appeared to do well at first later running into difficulties. And Bristol VRs have been associated with both success and failure in this environment.

Of course some services could never be viable, either because of their location or times of operation, such as evenings or Sundays when loadings are often poor. In these circumstances provision was made under the 1985 Act for local authorities to support, through a competitive tendering process, those services which may be uneconomic but nevertheless socially desirable. In such cases large vehicles are often called for, and in many instances Bristol VRs appear from both small and large operators. In a number of other situations small concerns have taken the opportunity to acquire former NBC group vehicles displaced by minibus schemes, only to embark on competitive ventures against the established operators!

The disposal programme for the National Bus Co differed from the privatisation of other former state-owned industries in that instead of offering the organisation for sale *en bloc* with the public given the chance to take a shareholding, subsidiary companies were sold individually, with the purchase frequently involving management and staff of the subsidiary concerned. Many of the NBC operating companies were divided before sale and, in retrospect, it is probably true to say that the first steps towards privatisation were taken as early as September 1981 when the Midland Red company (which some years earlier had lost much of its core with many services transferred to West Midlands PTE) was divided into five new operating companies. All initially retained 'Midland Red' in their title, although Midland Red (East) became 'Midland Fox' early in 1984.

Following the Midland Red split, there was speculation that other NBC subsidiaries – some of which had been enlarged by mergers in earlier years – would be similarly divided, but nothing more followed until 1 January 1983, when the Western National Omnibus Co was divided into smaller units, including four new operating companies. This was rapidly followed by the division of Hants & Dorset, East Kent/Maidstone & District, Bristol Omnibus and a succession of other NBC subsidiaries, with administration and engineering support itself provided by new, self-contained units formed from former head offices or central works until almost every NBC company had been restructured in this way. The hierarchy and bureaucracy of the established NBC structure was largely removed by this process and there is little doubt that each of the new, slimmer operating companies became more responsive to the local market. Moreover, the opportunity was taken to resurrect a number of older company titles such as Devon General, Hastings & District, North Western, Southern National and Wilts & Dorset, while many new names also appeared including Badgerline, Cambus, Cheltenham & Gloucester, Hampshire Bus, Luton & District, North Devon and Northumbria. Furthermore, operators seized the chance to dispense with the unpopular and drab NBC liveries in favour of new colours and fleetname styles. In some cases striking schemes such as the yellow and green of Badgerline, the red and blue of North Western and the red, grey and white of Northumbria emerged, while other operators opted to return to traditional colours, albeit in some cases applied in a new style. For example, East Kent returned to maroon and cream, and

Right:
The first NBC operating company to be privatised was Devon General, which was sold to its management in August 1986. A new livery of ivory and dark red was devised for its conventional buses, as worn here by Gardner-powered Nos 1208 and 1233 (the latter with 6LXC engine) at Exeter bus station. Devon General was among those operators which sought almost entirely to replace large buses with minibuses. By the beginning of 1993 the only 'big' bus remaining was a convertible VRT. *M. S. Curtis*

Centre right:
West Riding, incorporating Yorkshire Woollen, was purchased by its management in January 1987 to form the Caldaire group. During the following year, Yorkshire Woollen 829 (OWW 907P), a 1976 6LX-engined VRT/SL, pulls away from the Bradford Interchange for Dewsbury. With bold 'Yorkshire' fleetname, it retains pale green and cream livery as applied during the mid-1980s to NBC buses in the area so they would match those of the West Yorkshire PTE. *M. S. Curtis*

Bottom right:
When Hants & Dorset was divided in 1983, the name Wilts & Dorset was resurrected for the services which largely covered these counties. Wilts & Dorset subtly repainted its vehicles in Masons red — but in full NBC style — which conveyed the appearance of standard NBC poppy red but was brighter and didn't fade so rapidly. Upon the company's privatisation, Masons red continued as the basis of a revised and very attractive livery, as carried by No 3463 (GOG 654N), an MCW-bodied VRT/SL6G acquired second-hand from West Midlands PTE. It is seen at Swanage. *M. S. Curtis*

Right:
Further along the South Coast, competition raged in the Southampton area with Solent Blue Line, a new company controlled by Southern Vectis, having appeared in the city. This August 1987 photograph depicts crew-operated No 20 (JAH 400L), a former Eastern Counties and Cambus Series 2 VRT, in its two-tone blue and yellow livery. Soon afterwards Solent Blue Line took over the Hampshire Bus operations in the area. *M. S. Curtis*

Brighton & Hove adopted a new version of traditional red, cream and black, while Southdown restored its attractive apple green and cream livery and West Yorkshire returned to Tilling red and cream complete with traditional underlined gold fleetnames. Bristol VRTs appeared in all of these liveries, and many more besides, with the once ubiquitous NBC red and green shades rapidly banished, although some companies took longer than others to establish a new image before settling in the privately-owned sector.

The disposal of the NBC subsidiaries commenced in 1986. In August of that year Devon General became the first bus operating subsidiary to be privatised when purchased by its management team. By the end of the same year it had been followed into the private sector by Badgerline, Southern Vectis, Cheltenham & Gloucester, Maidstone & District, Cambus, PMT, South Midland, Midland Red West, Eastern National and Trent. All except Midland Red West had significant numbers of Bristol VRTs within their fleets and even that operator had acquired three examples from Bristol (City Line) by 1988.

Privatisation of NBC continued rapidly until April 1988, with Crosville Motor Services, Southern National, North Devon and London Country Bus (North East) among the last to be sold. The sale comprised 72 former subsidiaries, 52 of which were established bus operating

Right:
Potteries Motor Traction became simply PMT Ltd and was privatised at the end of 1986. This ultra-low VRT/SL3/501 (fleet No 669) with 74-seat bodywork stands at Uttoxeter in April 1988. Livery is bright red and yellow.
M. S. Curtis

ompanies. Of these, only Provincial and the /idland Red and London Country group ompanies were without VRs at the time of ecoming independent – but examples have nce appeared in these fleets, too.

Of the 52 bus companies sold, 37 were ought by their management or manage-nent and staff but some were subsequently cquired by other buyers. Almost immedi-tely, either by initial purchase or later akeover, a number of groups of companies ad begun to establish dominant positions. By ne end of 1988 these included Badgerline with 1,600 vehicles), Drawlane (1,050 vehi-les), Stagecoach (700 vehicles) and Transit oldings (550 vehicles). Where these circum-tances arose, and in order to promote and reserve the competition sought by Govern-nent, several investigations were conducted y the Monopolies & Mergers Commission with varying results) where neighbouring perators had returned to common owner-hip.

Among these groups was Badgerline oldings, which controlled both Badgerline formerly the Bristol Country Division of Bristol)mnibus) and City Line in Bristol (still officially nown as Bristol Omnibus Co Ltd), and which ad therefore become the direct successor to ne Bristol Tramways/Bristol Omnibus concern. y the early 1990s this group also included Midland Red West, Eastern National and its offshoot Thamesway, Wessex, Western National; and Brewers, South Wales Transport and United Welsh Coaches in Wales. By October 1992 the combined operational fleets had grown to over 2,300 vehicles, among which the second most numerous vehicle type (after Mercedes 608 minibuses), with 289 examples, was the Bristol VRT – 11 years after production of the type had ceased!

Another of the large groups was Stagecoach, but while a large number of Bristol VRTs was to be found in this organisation, the individual character of companies was largely eroded when Stagecoach applied its corporate livery of white with orange, red and blue stripes to every vehicle, regardless of which company it ran with. Transfers of vehicles, especially VRTs, have been common within the larger groups, and although the Stagecoach livery policy undoubtedly assists in the transfer of buses from company to company, once again some delightful liveries, such as those of Alder Valley, Cumberland, East Midland and Southdown, have again been lost, only a short time after replacing NBC's corporate colours.

Following the privatisation of NBC in England and Wales, came the announcement late in 1988 that the Scottish Bus Group would be similarly reorganised, and its subsidiaries

ight:
n the Northeast, Northern General remains a dominant perator. With 730 vehicles at ne time of its privatisation in May 1987, it was the largest perating subsidiary to be sold nder NBC's disposal rogramme. Still giving eoman front-line service espite being 13 years old when photographed, No 3410 JPT 910T) is a VRT/SL3/501 with CW highbridge bodywork. It seen racing towards the yne Bridge in September 992, destined for Hartlepool.
M. S. Curtis

Above:
City of Oxford has been subjected to substantial competition, but it has maintained its position in this busy university city. All of its double-deck buses bought new are of dual-door configuration, including No 484, a 70-seat VRT/SL3/6LXB new to the company in 1978. *M. S. Curtis*

Below:
National Welsh was another operator involved in intensely competitive activities. It absorbed the operations of several local municipal operators before difficulties caused National Welsh itself to cease trading early in 1992. The Red & White section of the business was saved, however, having been bought by Western Travel the previous year. Ultra-low VRT/SL LR722 (GTX 746W) is seen at Newport prior to the company's demise. *M. S. Curtis*

Bottom right:
One of the largest groups to emerge following the 1985 Transport Act was Stagecoach, which like NBC before it, imposed a standard livery policy for the vehicles of all its subsidiaries. United Counties was among the ex-NBC operators acquired by Stagecoach, and this scene at Bedford bus station in September 1989 illustrates how United Counties' deregulated livery of green, orange and cream had already been largely replaced by Stagecoach white with red, orange and blue stripes. Right, is No 944 (URP 944W), a VRT/SL3/6LXB new to the company in 1981, next to No 747 (LFJ 861W), a similar vehicle acquired from Devon General. On the left is No 641 (G641 EVV), one of the Alexander-bodied Leyland Olympians found throughout the Stagecoach group.
M. S. Curtis

sold-off, company by company. The first to go was SBG's smallest bus-operating company, Lowland, whose management and staff took control from August 1990, followed by Midland, and Eastern Scottish before the end of that year. By October 1991 the SBG sale was complete, with the final disposals involving Western (sold to its management and employees) and Clydeside 2000 (purchased by employees backed by Luton & District).

The Stagecoach group, which of course was based in Scotland, acquired the Bluebird Northern and Fife Scottish subsidiaries from the Scottish Bus Group. Then, using competitive tactics, it also took over the Highland company's services in the Inverness area – through Stagecoach's Inverness Traction company – before merging this operation with Bluebird Northern. Stagecoach had already become an established VRT operator, and Bristol VRTs were also acquired in Scotland by Kelvin Central, Lowland and Strathtay, the latter's VRs being transferred from its new owner Yorkshire Traction. Further examples could be found with a number of smaller operators, dispelling at last the notion that VRs could not be successfully run north of the border.

Buses belonging to the state-owned bus companies were not the only vehicles to undergo a change in ownership through company restructuring. Among the less dramatic provisions of the 1985 Transport Act was a requirement that the bus undertakings of non-metropolitan district councils, and the bus operations of the Transport Executives in the metropolitan areas outside London, be transferred to new companies which, while remaining in the ownership of the authority concerned, would be at arm's length. This was to demonstrate their independence and allow them freedom to compete against other bus companies for both commercial and tendered operations. The provision was intended to achieve a situation where the bus industry as a whole was fully deregulated, competitive and free from direct public ownership, and among the local authorities affected were those whose fleets contained significant numbers of Bristol VRs such as Burnley & Pendle, Cardiff, Great Yarmouth, Lincoln and Northampton.

Full deregulation took effect from 26 October 1986 and from that time stable and previously protected service networks have been subject to competition from rival operators. Many examples of intense competition have been seen, including between former state-owned NBC operators, ex-NBC and council companies and, in a great many situ-

Right:
Carrying both East Midland and Mansfield & District fleetnames, Bristol VRT/SL 222 (KKY 222W) prepares to leave Newark bus station in July 1991. East Midland was among the last NBC companies to be privatised in February 1988, bought initially by its management but later acquired by Stagecoach. The attractive two-tone green and ivory livery carried by No 222 was therefore soon to be swept away by Stagecoach white with stripes. *M. S. Curtis*

Right:
Yet another company to regain its individual identity, only to lose it again when acquired by Stagecoach, was Cumberland Motor Services. Seen in Carlisle in August 1987 is highbridge-bodied VRT No 1450 (LHG 450T), new to Ribble in 1979 but transferred with the Carlisle area services prior to privatisation (Ribble having also later joined the Stagecoach group). Cumberland's short-lived red and sandstone is carried in this view. *S. J. Butler*

Centre right:
Representative of dozens of Bristol VRs acquired by small independent or private operators, and in many cases used competitively against former NBC companies, is UGR 694R, which joined Bakers of Weston-super-Mare as its No 67 during 1989. It was formerly Northumbria 515. Just visible behind is another VRT, this time an ex-West Midlands PTE MCW-bodied example. *M. S. Curtis*

Bottom right:
Southend Transport, whilst never purchasing Bristol VRs new, amassed a significant fleet of second-hand examples from various sources during 1992. These have been used to compete in Southend against Thamesway, a Badgerline group company which in contrast has replaced VRs with minibuses. No 307 (WTU 473W), loading for its next journey in this January 1993 view, was new as Crosville DVG 473. *M. S. Curtis*

ations, involving small private concerns which have attacked established services.

In a great number of clashes between operators, the Bristol VR has been prominent. Many examples sold, either displaced by minibuses or simply surplus to requirements, have been turned against their former owners, and there have been a number of locations where former NBC companies have faced competition from ex-NBC VRs from elsewhere. Moreover, the general reduction in new vehicle orders as a result of the new environment has further encouraged the retention of older economical and flexible vehicles such as the VR, although a few operators have set about the replacement of all large buses by minibuses. The frequency with which VRTs have been engaged in competitive ventures has nevertheless been remarkable and could never have been foreseen when this model was in production.

Casualties among operators have of course resulted from such competition, but while their owners may have contracted, the vehicles involved have often been disposed of for service elsewhere. This has led to some unexpected developments, such as Southend Transport in Essex acquiring the first of a large fleet of VRTs in 1992, and the return of Bristol VRs to several Scottish companies. Such activity has caused considerable operational interest, whilst further adding to the variety of liveries worn by this model!

Stability in the bus industry has inevitably been reduced, with an unprecedented shift in company boundaries having been witnessed since 1986; and the demise of operators such as National Welsh (after earlier expansion)

Below:
Lincolnshire Road Car Co was purchased by Yorkshire Traction, and like so many former NBC companies has endured extensive competition from a range of other operators. With deregulation the company changed its fleetname from 'Lincolnshire' to 'Road Car' — as carried by No 1968 (SVL 178W), a Bristol/ECW VRT/SL built in 1981 and captured on film 10 years later at Lincoln. *M. S. Curtis*

serves to emphasise that long term predictions of events can no longer be straightforward. Nevertheless, many operators have demonstrated they can sustain rivalry from competitors and continue operations undeterred.

The VRT has shown it is very well suited to the new operating environment, and its success in competitive activities against both conventional buses (including other VRs) or minibuses stands testimony to its sound basic design that evolved from the 1960s. And while bus passengers sometimes endure disruption and confusion, Bristol's VR double-decker provides some degree of reassurance and continuity by maintaining public services despite changing operating conditions.

Above right:
Yorkshire Traction also took control of the Dundee-based Strathtay Scottish Omnibuses, which became the only former Scottish Bus Group company not sold to a Scottish buyer. During the summer of 1991, seven Leyland 501-engined Bristol VRTs from the parent fleet received Strathtay's blue, orange and white livery at Barnsley. They were then transferred to Scotland for use on school contracts — but in fact they were employed regularly on all-day service. A year later they returned south to Yorkshire. SB1 (KKY 834P) is depicted here in full Strathtay livery. *S. D. V. Thomas*

Right:
Among the most remote Bristol VRs must be those belonging to Lowland Omnibuses. No 855 (NDL 655R), posed here at Galashiels specially for this book during June 1993, symbolises the VR in Scotland. Despite the VR's many difficulties north of the border, Lowland (a direct successor to Eastern Scottish, which received the first production VRTs in 1968) successfully operates a trio of VRT3s acquired from Southern Vectis. In doing so it helps to banish the myth that this model is unsuitable for Scottish service. *M. S. Curtis*

12

New Roles: New Owners

The acquisition of double-deck buses for further use after withdrawal by their first owners is not new, and most certainly is not unique to the Bristol VR model. The varied and widespread uses to which Bristol's Vertical Rear-engined range of double-deckers have been put after sale has, nonetheless, resulted in some interesting new roles for many VRs, whether for continued use as passenger-carrying vehicles with other operators, or for quite different purposes. VRs have accordingly been seen not only in new operators' colours, but adapted for various tasks including private works transport, travelling showrooms, mobile churches, circus transport and caravans. In addition, a surprising number have enjoyed extended lives working overseas on both sightseeing and conventional bus duties.

It will be remembered that as early as 1971 the first of a large number of VRTs were offered for disposal by the Scottish Bus Group, and while most passed to NBC operators, two moved to an independent concern and another was sold to a contractor. Moreover, many of the Standerwick VRLs saw further use on tourist and sightseeing work, both at home and abroad, while one example became private transport for a football team.

In the heyday of the National Bus Company, a process of cascading buses developed. This was often as a consequence of varying passenger demand for double-deckers being identified through market analysis projects, which caused considerable numbers of Bristol VRTs to be transferred between operators across the country. In general, NBC's Bristol/ECW VRTs are thought of as being highly standardised, but some interesting variations of the basic design were involved in such transfers. These included London Country's highbridge-bodied VRTs moving to Bristol Omnibus, to become the only Bristol-built double-deckers in that fleet not constructed to lowheight configuration; rare flat-front, dual-door VRT/SLs were moved from Southdown, again to Bristol, where they joined similar vehicles on Bristol City Services; and ultra-low bodywork VRTs (including some with Leyland 501 engines) were sent from Yorkshire Traction to Western/Southern National, which had built up a fleet of standard, lowheight Bristol VRTs. Further VRTs from East Midland, Northern General, Oxford-South Midland, PMT, United Auto and West Riding were also dispersed among NBC's various West Country fleets. MCW-bodied VRTs from West Midlands PTE, together with East Lancs-bodied examples from South Yorkshire PTE (both featuring rear engine bustles), found their way into several Welsh NBC fleets, as did some of the

Right:
When the Scottish Bus Group decided to dispose of its entire stock of Bristol VRTs, most were exchanged for NBC Lodekkas, but a pair of ex-Western SMT examples found their way into the fleet of Osborne's of Tollesbury, Essex. NAG 588G, formerly Western 2237 and still wearing that operator's colours, is about to depart from Colchester bus station for its new home as Osborne's No 26. *The late R. F. Mack.*

ex-Tayside Alexander-bodied VRT/LLs. There were also many more instances where Bristol VRTs moved between operators during the NBC era.

Following the privatisation of the state-owned operators and the establishment of new groups of companies, further cascading of vehicles and transfers within groups have remained commonplace. As already mentioned in Chapter 11, this and the effects of deregulation have further encouraged significant levels of dealing and trading in vehicles, especially VRs, between bus operators from all sectors,

The export success of the VRT was extremely limited, and a left-hand drive version of the model was never offered. A number of VRTs and VRLs have nevertheless been sold abroad for further service. Several have found their way to Canada and the United States, including a small batch of VRLs used on city sightseeing work in Chicago, one of which was still running in 1989. Australia, too, has seen both VRLs and VRTs at work, including an ex-Reading VRT/LL operated on tours of Melbourne, while a small fleet of VRT/SLs joined London Transport Tours of Perth, Western Australia.

Two attempts have been made to rebuild the VRT in left-hand drive form for American use. The first involved Porter's Bus/America Inc, an operator and dealer that imported a variety of British double-deckers into the USA, including Bristol Lodekkas and VRs. In 1983 a proposal was made to rebuild VRTs with not only left-hand drive but also new mechanical

Right:
As requirements for one-person operated double-deckers changed from one subsidiary company to another, NBC cascaded VRTs between fleets, while further VRTs were acquired second-hand from non-NBC operators where demand warranted increased use of larger vehicles. Leading a rather quieter life in Wales than when operating for Sheffield Corporation and later South Yorkshire PTE, OWE 280K, an East Lancs-bodied VRT, had become Crosville HVG936 when photographed at Llanidloes. *C. L. Caddy*

Right:
A very different role from that for which it was built was adopted by this Bristol VRL coach. Originally Standerwick No 64 (OCK 64K), it was amongst those sold to Tyne & Wear PTE, but in October 1983 was exported to Australia where it joined Harmer's Fun Decker Coachlines operation in Melbourne, carrying licence plate BSW.803. *Greg Travers*

Centre right:
A new role with its original owner is demonstrated by this VRT, viewed in Central Bristol during October 1987. The Bristol Omnibus Co (by this time trading as City Line) had converted EHU 362K, one of its original dual-door VRTs, to become a driver training unit. Revised driver licensing regulations were introduced from April 1991, which resulted in double-deck training buses generally being replaced by single-deck vehicles for tuition and testing purposes. *M. S. Curtis*

Bottom right:
XRD 19K was one of the first Reading 'Jumbo' Bristol VRT/LLs with Northern Counties coachwork which, upon withdrawal, found its way to Red Bus Services of Exeter, Devon. It was finished in a red and cream livery which to some extent restored its original Reading image, but is here awaiting another buyer (during August 1986) while in the hands of Father Green, the Dorset-based used bus dealer. *M. S. Curtis*

components, including a Detroit diesel engine and Allison automatic transmission, to be promoted in America as a 'remanufactured' model known as the 'Ascent I'. Some interesting publicity was produced which contained an official ECW photograph of an early Scottish VRT, printed in reverse to demonstrate how such a bus might appear! One vehicle, an early flat-screen VRT new to Midland General as No 317 (BNU 681G), was actually rebuilt to left-hand drive in Britain as a prototype for the Ascent I, but it retained its Gardner engine and stairs behind what had become the entrance. Unfortunately, by the time it was delivered in 1984 to Porter's Bus in Minneapolis, Porter's had ceased trading and the VRT (which remained unique) was purchased by the nearby Richfield Bus Co, which already owned two Bristol VRL/LH double-deckers.

A similar project followed in 1987, this time involving the Bristol Ominbus Co (now trading as City Line), which had arranged to extensively rebuild five of its 1973 batch of dual-door, Series 2 VRT/SL6Gs to left-hand drive for use by Spirit of '76 Tours of Washington DC. Painted red, they were fitted with low-profile wheels and tyres to reduce overall height, but while four of these were nearing completion – the first to be converted having already crossed the Atlantic – the scheme was hurriedly dropped! It had been discovered that under American liability legislation, the manu-

Right:
The idea of 're-manufacturing' Bristol VRTs as the Ascent 1 model for use in the United States of America never progressed beyond the rebuilding of former Midland General BNU 681G, a 1969 VRT/SL with ECW body, to left-hand drive. It is seen (with new licence No 2C 5358) with the Richfield Bus Co of Minneapolis, during June 1986 while operating a circular tourist route in Chisholm, Minnesota. The staircase remains in its original position despite the reversed cab and entrance. *David Hunt*

Below right:
Another abortive attempt to rebuild VRTs to left-hand drive for use in the USA is demonstrated by LHW 799L, one of five Bristol Omnibus (City Line) VRT/SLs intended for use by Spirit of '76 Tours of Washington DC, whose red livery is carried. As its conversion neared completion, the project was abandoned owing to difficulties presented by American liability laws. The low profile wheels and tyres are of particular interest as a means of reducing overall height. *M. S. Curtis*

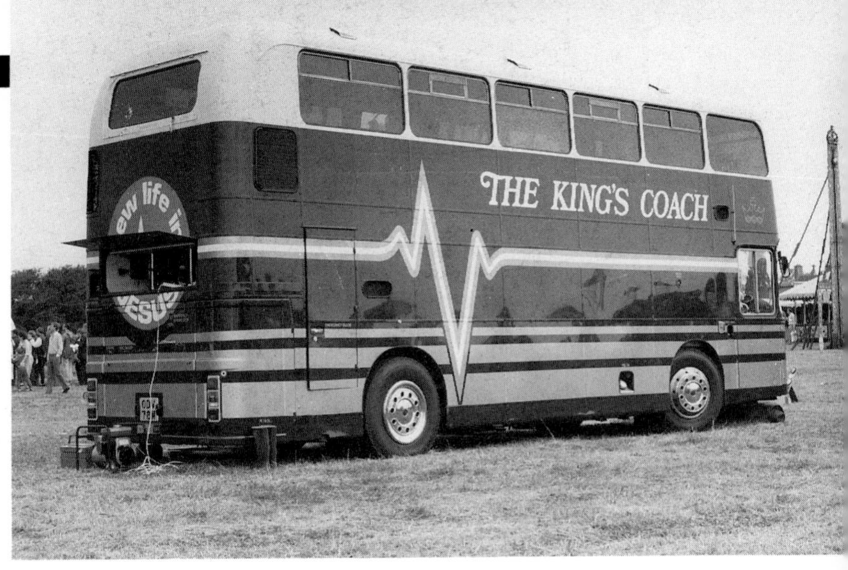

Right:
Among several interesting buses acquired by the Roffey Place Christian Training Centre, Horsham, to carry 'The King's Coach' name, was ODV 78M, the prototype Series 3 VRT previously operated by Western National. Immaculately finished in dark blue, white and gold, this bus became a travelling exhibition and hospitality unit, and is seen in this role at Yeovil during the summer of 1986. *M. S. Curtis*

facturer could be liable for very large sums of money if compensation ever had to be paid following loss or injury involving anyone riding on or operating these vehicles – and as Bristol Commercial Vehicles had already closed, Bristol Omnibus would probably have been regarded as the manufacturer. This situation prevented the project from proceeding, so Bristol Ominbus arranged for these vehicles to be sold and dismantled – although a mystery surrounds exactly what happened to them after sale and it is rumoured some may have survived, eventually entering service in the Middle East!

With so many VRs still required for service in Britain, there is a limit to the numbers released for sale to either new operators or for other purposes. Naturally, of those Bristol VRs that have been withdrawn, some are considered suitable only for scrapping or cannibalisation for spare parts, having reached the end of their operational lives. Considerable demand remains, though, for those which are offered for further service. And, gradually, VRs are entering the ranks of preserved buses, ensuring examples of Bristol's VR design will be saved for posterity, long after their revenue-earning capabilities have passed.

Right:
An aspect of bus operation which is of growing importance is 'park & ride', with several of the more successful schemes having, at some stage, employed Bristol VRs. Cheltenham Park & Ride involves a frequent Saturday service from the racecourse to the town centre, with former Bristol Omnibus dual-door VRT/SLs used to maintain this well-patronised facility. PHY 693S (left) with LEU 266P (behind) await their next journeys. Like many such schemes, this service is provided on a contracted basis, in this case by Circle Line — whose normal dark green and cream is carried but with the addition of 'Park & Ride' lettering. *M. S. Curtis*

Appendices

Above:
VRX prototype HHW 933D, wearing green 'Gloucester' livery while in Metz, France during 1967. *Bristol*

Above:
In 1967 a further experimental chassis was built to Long wheelbase, High frame (VRLH) configuration. Its frame design differed from the earlier low frame prototypes and was the first chassis fitted with a spring parking brake. Powered by a Leyland engine, this chassis never received bodywork.
Bristol

1 Bristol VRL Customers

	VRL/LL/(NX)	VRL/SL(VRX)	VRL/LH	Total
BCV	1	2	1	4
Johannesburg			14	14
Pretoria			11	11
Standerwick			30	30
	1	*2*	*56*	*59*

2 Bristol VRL Bodywork

	VRL/LL/(NX)	VRL/SL (VRX)	VRL/LH	Total
ECW		2	30	32
Bus Bodies (SA)			25	25
Not bodied	1		1	2
	1	*2*	*56*	*59*

3 Bristol VRT Series 1 Customers

	VRT/SL	VRT/LL	VRT/LH	Total
Alexander (Midland)	15			15
Brighton Hove & District	10			10
Central SMT	20			20
Eastern Counties	15			15
Eastern National	5			5
Lincolnshire	5			5
Merseyside PTE			25	25
Midland General	6			6
Scottish Omnibuses	10	25		35
Stockport	10			10
Southern Vectis	2			2
Thames Valley	13			13
United Auto	20			20
United Counties	8			8
West Yorkshire group	49			49
Western National	10			10
Western SMT	39			39
	237	*25*	*25*	*287*

4 Bristol VRT Series I Bodywork

	VRT/SL	VRT/LL	VRT/LH	Total
ECW	227	25		252
East Lancs			24	24
Smithfield	1			1
Not bodied	9		1	10
	237	*25*	*25*	*287*

Above:
York-West Yorkshire No 3933 (YWU 454G) races away from York railway station wearing Tilling red and cream colours. Shallow sliding windows and a 'T'-style destination display were specified by the operator. *M. S. Curtis*

Above:
Many operators routinely fuel and wash their buses at the end of their working day. Driving through the Neptune automatic bus wash at Weymouth in the mid-1980s is a Series 2 VRT/SL. *M. S. Curtis*

Above:
REH 815M, another ultra-low VRT, this time in NBC green livery. Despite carrying Crosville fleetnames and allocated fleet No DVG 615, this vehicle is actually Potteries Motor Traction 615 . It was photographed in Liverpool during September 1975.
M. S. Curtis

5 Bristol VRT Series 2 Customers

	VRT/SL	VRT/LL	VRT/LH	Total
Alder/Thames Valley	17			17
Bristol Ominbus	32			32
Cardiff	20			20
Crosville	12			12
Cumberland	6			6
Dept of Environment	1			1
Devon General	9			9
East Midlands	30			30
East Yorkshire	18			18
Eastern Counties	61			61
Eastern National	26			26
Gelligaer	3			3
Hants & Dorset	28			28
Hutchings & Cornelius	1			1
Lincolnshire	13			13
Maidstone & District	61			61
Mansfield District	13			13
Merseyside PTE	50		35	85
Midland General	7			7
Northern General	4			4
Oxford	26			26
PMT	31			31
Reading		31		31
Ribble	23			23
SELNEC PTE	25			25
Sheffield	18			18
Southdown	70			70
Southern Vectis	26			26
Trent	25			25
United Auto	28			28
United Counties	78			78
West Midlands PTE	200			200
West Riding	19			19
West Yorkshire group	19			19
Western National	36			36
Yorkshire Traction	33			33
	1,069	*31*	*35*	*1,135*

6 Bristol VRT Series 2 Bodywork

	VRT/SL	VRT/LL	VRT/LH	Total
ECW	798			798
East Lancs	68		35	103
Metro-Cammell Weymann	200			200
Northern Counties	3	31		34
	1,069	*31*	*35*	*1,135*

Above:
Just when it appeared that NBC's corporate liveries had reached the ultimate in dreariness, some operators started painting their vehicles in all-over NBC red or green – without any white relief whatsoever! Originally Yorkshire Traction 851, OWE 851R, had become Southern National 608, with ultra-low ECW body painted completely in leaf green, when photographed at Bridport in April 1985.
M. S. Curtis

Above:
Bristol VRs in Bristol. These two dual-door, centre staircase VRT/SLs are at work in the city that gave their chassis manufacturer its name. No 5003 (EHU 362K), an indigenous Bristol Omnibus example, overtakes No 5207 (WUF 535K), acquired second-hand from Southdown.
A. R. Macfarlane

7 Bristol VRT Series 3 Customers

	VRT/SL	VRT/LL	VRT/LH	Total
Alder Valley	100			100
Bristol Omnibus group	171			171
Burnley & Pendle	24			24
Cardiff	97			97
Cleveland Transit	15			15
Crosville	231			231
Cumberland	32			32
East Kent	70			70
East Midland	84			84
East Yorkshire	61			61
Eastern Counties	144			144
Eastern National	78			78
Great Yarmouth	16			16
Hants & Dorset	122			122
AERE Harwell	7			7
Lincoln	14	7		21
Lincolnshire	52			52
London Country	15			15
Maidstone & District	95			95
A Mayne & Son	5			5
Midland General	16			16
National/Western Welsh (Red & White)	56			56
Northampton	42			42
Northern General	112			112
Oxford	71			71
PMT	100			100
Reading		19		19
Rhymney Valley	3			3
Ribble	60			60
Sijthoff Pers	1			1
South Wales Transport	91			91
Southdown	154			154
Southern Vectis	42			42
Stevensons of Uttoxeter	2			2
Tayside		25		25
Trent	57			57
United Auto	156			156
United Counties	132			132
West Riding	85			85
West Yorkshire group	102			102
Western National group	189			189
Yorkshire Traction	73			73
Yorkshire Woollen	24			24
	3,001	*51*		*3,052*

Above:
Alder Valley 985 (CJH 125V) is viewed at London Victoria in April 1980, just after entry into service. It features the final slider and hopper window designs for ECW bodied VRTs.
G. R. Mills

Above:
The world's largest gathering of open top buses occurs each year for the Epsom Derby. Eastern Counties OT351 (OCK 995K), which was Ribble 1995 prior to conversion, approaches the racecourse.
M. S. Curtis

Above:
United 658 (BHN 758N), a Series 2 VRT/SL after conversion to permanent open top, at Scarborough in 1986.
Kevin Lane

8 Bristol VRT Series 3 Bodywork

	VRT/SL	VRT/LL	VRT/LH	Total
ECW	2,769			2,769
Alexander	107	25		132
East Lancs	27	7		34
Northern Counties	15	19		34
Willowbrook	83			83
	3,001	*51*		*3,052*

9 Bristol VRT Production Totals

	Series 1	Series 2	Series 3	Total
Alder/Thames Valley	13	17	100	130
Alexander (Midland)	15			15
Bristol Omnibus group		32	171	203
Burnley & Pendle			24	24
Cardiff		20	97	117
Central SMT	20			20
Cleveland Transit			15	15
Crosville		12	231	243
Cumberland		6	32	38
Dept of Environment		1		1
East Kent			70	70
East Midlands/Mansfield District		43	84	127
East Yorkshire		18	61	79
Eastern Counties	15	61	144	220
Eastern National	5	26	78	109
Gelligaer/Rhymney Valley		3	3	6
Great Yarmouth			16	16
Hants & Dorset		28	122	150
AERE Harwell			7	7
Hutchings & Cornelius		1		1
Lincoln			21	21
Lincolnshire	5	13	52	70
London Country			15	15
Maidstone & District		61	95	156
A Mayne & Son			5	5
Merseyside PTE	25	85		110
National/Western Welsh (Red & White)		56		56
Northampton			42	42
Northern General		4	112	116
Oxford		26	71	97
PMT		31	100	131
Reading		31	19	50
Ribble		23	60	83
Scottish Omnibuses	35			35
SELNEC PTE/Stockport	10	25		35
Sheffield		18		18
Sijthoff Pers			1	1
South Wales Transport			91	91

Above:
West Yorkshire 1724 at Bradford in September 1988, wearing a revival of pre-NBC Tilling red and cream livery. *M. S. Curtis*

	Series 1	Series 2	Series 3	Total
Southdown/ Brighton Hove & District	10	70	154	234
Southern Vectis	2	26	42	70
Stevensons of Uttoxeter			2	2
Tayside			25	25
Trent/Midland General	6	32	73	111
United Auto	20	28	156	204
United Counties	8	78	132	218
West Midlands PTE		200		200
West Riding/Yorkshire Woollen		19	109	128
West Yorkshire group	49	19	102	170
Western National group	10	45	189	244
Western SMT	39			39
Yorkshire Traction		33	73	106
	287	*1,135*	*3,052*	*4,474*

Above:
A dramatic red, grey and white livery was chosen by Northumbria (a company formed by the forced division of United Automobile Services). VRT/SL 587 (APT 820W) displays this stunning scheme in Grainer Street, Newcastle-upon-Tyne. *M. S. Curtis*

Below:
The 'Bristol VR' badge was introduced in 1966 and since then has been recognised by millions of bus passengers who have seen it fixed on or near the radiator grille. The badge has also become familiar to other road users — the chances are most British motorists have followed a VR at one time or another — since a similar 'Bristol VR' badge has appeared on the rear engine cover of every new Bristol VRT. *M. S. Curtis*

Left:
During 1973-74, 11 ECW-bodied VRTs for various NBC subsidiary companies were constructed with experimental split-level entrances, intended to assist elderly and disabled passengers by reducing the first step from 14in to 11in. One such vehicle was Western National's 1072, which illustrates this arrangement. Step layouts to this pattern became common on all types of bus in later years. *M. S. Curtis*

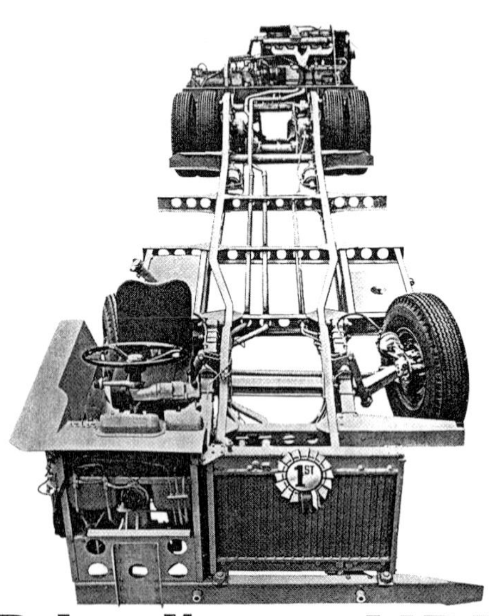

Bristol's new V.R.T.

Another winner from the Lodekka stable

Here it is – the first quantity production double-decker chassis from Bristol since the Lodekka (we don't have to tell you how successful that was – and is!)
The new VRT with Vertical Rear Transverse engine has so many outstanding features, including its very competitive price.

Choice of Engines
Gardner 6 LX or 6 LXB ; Leyland 0.680.

Simple Maintenance
The Bristol VRT chassis has only eight grease points. Engine and gearbox unit enclosed by moulded G.R.P. structure permits easy access to all parts of the power unit and gearbox.

Clean Comfortable Cab
Floor, offside and instrument facia are moulded from G.R.P., with controls placed to reduce driver fatigue.

Stainless Steel Brake Piping

Drop Axle yet Removable Differential

Optimum Performance
Road speeds of 63 m.p.h. and gradient ability of 1 in 4 can be achieved.

Excellent Choice of Optional Alternatives
The Bristol VRT chassis having the engine and gearbox unit mounted transversely at the extreme rear of the chassis caters for double or single deck body work.
Please write for more information.

BRISTOL

BRISTOL COMMERCIAL VEHICLES LTD
BRISLINGTON BRISTOL BS4 3LD
TELEPHONE BRISTOL 77613

Top:
A line-up of nine Bristol VRs awaiting their next tour of duty, at Badgerline's Kensington depot, Bath. Nearest the camera is No 5509 (KOU 795P).
M. S. Curtis

Above:
A Bristol VRT advertisement which appeared during 1968 in *Buses* magazine.